# MUSIC
# FUNDAMENTALS

# MUSIC
# FUNDAMENTALS

## A Guide to Musical Understanding

by Howard A. Murphy
*Manhattan School of Music*
*Teachers College, Columbia University (Emeritus)*

with the assistance of
John F. Park

San Francisco

Chandler Publishing Company

*Sole Distributors to the Music Trade*

Sam Fox Publishing Company New York

*New York*

# Preface

This guide to musical understanding through a study of music fundamentals is planned to meet the interests of the general reader and of the college student. It is designed on the premise that increased knowledge about music and its structure enhances one's enjoyment of it. It is not, however, intended to be a replacement for the music itself, just as the reading about music is not equivalent to the appreciation of it.

It is hoped that the organization of the book in the form of questions and answers, which are arranged in a logical sequence, will stimulate additional questions in the reader's mind, encouraging him to do further study. It must be stressed that this book is intended to be used as a guide rather than as a dictionary or encyclopedia of music.

The author is indebted to James F. Leisy for his helpful suggestions; to Charles W. Walton, David Barnett, Mary Lenom, and Ruth van Doren for their critical reading of the manuscript in its early stages; to his understanding and cooperative publisher; and to his students and colleagues who have through the years perhaps unknowingly contributed to the pages that follow.

Acknowledgement is made also to the Kansas City Life Insurance Company for permission to use the Frequency Range Chart in Section VIII, and to John F. Park for the preparation of all the other material in Section VIII, and for his invaluable and timely assistance in the final revision of the manuscript.

Howard A. Murphy

New York

# Contents

# MUSIC
# FUNDAMENTALS

# SECTION ONE | Musical Understanding

When listening to music, the hearer receives many different impressions which fuse into a unified whole. Naturally, he seldom tries to separate or analyze these different impressions. He enjoys the total effect of the music. His reaction is a basic sensuous enjoyment of musical tones arranged in interesting rhythms. If he is aware of any one of the elements which make up the whole, he probably listens to the melody or is conscious of the rhythm.

Yet music consists of many components, all of which are interesting in themselves. Moreover, increased knowledge about music —if properly used—enhances the listener's enjoyment, just as knowledge of the technical aspects of games increases the spectator's pleasure. A football, baseball, or basketball game means much more when the spectator knows something about how the game is played. This knowledge of technique, whether it be in sports or in the arts, involves our minds in addition to our senses and emotions. In other words, using our minds as well as our ears when listening to music increases our enjoyment of the sound and our emotional reactions to it. The intellectual and sensuous approaches to music are complementary, not contradictory. Neither excludes the other; both increase enjoyment. We should be able both to sing or whistle a melody and to understand something of its structure if we wish to derive the greatest pleasure from it.

Music has been defined as the language of feeling or as "wordless poetry." As a language it has an organization and a vocabulary. Originally it was only a "spoken" language, but man eventually developed a system for writing it which records its essentials.

Music has also been called "frozen architecture," the composer being the architect, the performer, the builder. The musical score of the composer-architect is the blueprint from which the performer-builder creates the sounds we hear. An understanding of this blueprint enables us both to enjoy music as listeners and to recreate it as performers.

But there is an additional reason for the listener being musically literate—the fact that music is an art that exists exclusively in time. A work of music is like a chain of pearls whose appreciation depends upon a grasp of the whole as well as of the parts. The enjoyment of music at any one moment is only partial. The beauty of the moment is dependent on the whole composition. Fuller enjoyment includes the ability to hear the connection between what has already been heard and what is being heard. Hence, the auditor resembles a person who must view a large painting inch by inch. For the painting to "make sense," this viewer must recall what he has seen before. For one who listens to music, this sense of the past is developed by an understanding of musical structure or design known as *form*. For the listener an understanding of form may be compared to a map of an unknown country. Through its use he orients himself to the tonal country he is exploring.

Granted that an understanding of musical structure enhances enjoyment, are the technical aspects of music too complicated to be easily mastered? The answer is definitely "No." The facts of musical structure are quite simple if they are learned in a framework of familiar melodies and are properly related.

As you read the following pages, you will be introduced gradually to what musical tones are, how they are notated, and finally to the ways composers combine tones in melodies and chords and arrange their musical ideas in satisfying patterns. You need no knowledge of music beyond what you already have. But it is important that you apply what you learn as you *listen* to music. Listening implies thinking *and* hearing. Through the use of both mind and ears, you can discover the true beauty and meaning of music for your own enjoyment and enrichment.

The material presented in the following pages is necessarily somewhat technical since the description of any organized field of knowledge must use that field's vocabulary. Painting cannot be described in terms of music, nor physics in terms of chemistry. Only confusion results from too much "translating" or diluting of technical material. Hence, we shall use the technical vocabulary of music to present the essential facts about it.

In your reading you will use your own musical experience as background, for actually you already know much more about music than you realize. You will have additional questions; try to answer them by reasoning deductively from the material presented, which is designed to be used as a *guide* rather than as a dictionary or an encyclopedia. Each section concludes with a summary that you may wish to read first, especially if the material is somewhat familiar to you. You may wish to refer frequently to the Glossary in Section VIII for an explanation of musical terms. You will find the Frequency Range Chart on p. 87 helpful in comparing the pitch range of musical media. The Historical Chart on p. 84 will provide you with a frame of reference for the principal musical forms and representative composers of historical periods. You will find in the Bibliography a selection of reading material that will aid in increasing your musical understanding.

Finally, it is important for you to know the plan of the piano keyboard, either by *sight* (from a diagram—see the Frequency Range Chart, p. 87) or by *touch* (from playing). The piano keyboard embodies an organization of the tones used in music; and therefore it will be helpful for you to know the keyboard plan. Gradually learn to think about music in terms of the keyboard, and if you have access to a piano, try to play the examples. By doing so, you will translate abstract facts into concrete aural realities. However, in music as a language, the best judge is always the *ear*. Develop your ability to listen to music intelligently. Then its organization and meaning as a language will become increasingly clear to you.

# SECTION TWO | Musical Tone

Sound and silence are the basic raw materials of music. An architect designs his structures in terms of masses and voids of physical material; a composer designs his structures in terms of masses and voids of sonorous material. The composer communicates through the skillful use of his material—musical tone. Our first step toward musical understanding is to define *musical tone*, for tones are to a musician what bricks are to a builder or what words are to an author.

**1. What is Tone?** Music is an art perceived through the ear. The scientific bases of music are the laws of sound collectively known as *acoustics*. Sound is a sensation received through the ear. It is caused by the vibrations of elastic or tremulous bodies such as strings, columns of air, membranes, vocal chords, or metal bars. The vibrations of these bodies are transmitted to the ear through the air.

A *tone* may be defined as a sound produced by a regular and comparatively simple number of vibrations per second. All other sounds are noises, though tone and noise are actually relative terms. The three characteristics of tones are: *pitch, intensity,* and *quality*. *Duration,* or the length of time a tone continues to sound, is sometimes included as a fourth characteristic. However, duration refers to the length, not to the structure of a tone.

**2. What is Pitch?**   Tones are said to sound "high" or "low" in relation to each other. This contrast in sound is due to their *pitch*. Pitch is determined by the frequency of the vibration of sound waves. Difference in pitch is caused by the difference in the frequencies or rates of vibration. A "low" tone has a lower frequency of vibration than a "high" tone.

The average person can hear tones within a range from 16 vibrations per second to 20,000 vibrations per second. Our singing range from low bass to high soprano is from approximately 82 to about 1300 vibrations. The piano extends from 27 to 4186, the organ from 16 to 4186, and the orchestra from 32 to approximately 4000 vibrations. (See the Frequency Range Chart, p. 87.) The standard pitch today, fixed by international agreement, is 440 vibrations per second for the A near the center of the piano keyboard. The basic difference between a musical tone and a noise can be shown by comparing the sound of a kettle drum, which has definite pitch, with that of a bass drum, whose pitch is indefinite.

**3. What is Intensity?**   Tones are said to be "loud" or "soft," depending upon the strength of the sensations received by the ear. This characteristic is the *intensity* or volume of a tone. It is caused by the width or *amplitude* of its vibrations. If a violin string is plucked forcefully and then lightly, it is obvious that the string is displaced more by the strong than by the weak plucking. The ear will notice a difference in the intensity (volume) of the repeated sound, though the pitch remains the same. This experiment shows the difference between pitch and intensity since pitch is caused by the frequency of the vibrations and intensity by their amplitude. Remember that "high" and "low" refer to the pitch of a tone, while "loud" and "soft" refer to its intensity or volume. Composers indicate on their musical scores the degree of intensity desired. These indications are called *dynamic markings*. (See the Glossary.)

**4. What is Quality?**   The third characteristic of a tone refers to the difference between tones of the same pitch and intensity that are produced by different instruments or voices—that element of tone which makes a violin sound different from a clarinet. This difference is called tone color, timbre, tone quality, or simply *quality*. Quality is the difference in sound between the same tone produced by different instruments.

Quality is due to the fact that an elastic or tremulous medium, for example, a violin string, when set in motion vibrates in two ways: as a whole and also in parts. Each of these parts or segments produces a faint additional tone differing in pitch from the primary tone, but mingled with it. Thus, the tone we hear is a composite. Its component tones are called partial tones, or simply *partials*. The fundamental tone, though produced by the whole string, is called the first partial, and the other partials are called *overtones*. The overtones produced by string or wind instruments are also known as *harmonics*, and collectively are called the *harmonic series*, or the "chord of nature." Thus, the terms *partials, overtones,* and *harmonics* all refer to this series of tones produced by segments of the vibrating medium.

The number of partials present in a tone depends upon three factors: the producing instrument, the pitch of the tone, and the loudness of the tone. A "pure" tone without any partials is a poor tone, having a thin, colorless sound. The number and relative strength of partials sounding with any tone determines its *quality*. For example, among orchestral instruments, the oboe tone contains the most overtones, while the flute tone has the fewest. Consequently, the oboe has a rich, vibrant quality in contrast to the clear, pure tone of the flute. It should be remembered that overtones are present in all musical tones heard, whether sung or played.

## Summary—Musical Tone

Music is both a science and an art. Its physical basis is the science of acoustics. Broadly speaking, a musical *tone* has a regular number of vibrations per second, while a noise has an irregular or indefinite number. Acoustically, a tone has three properties: *pitch*, *intensity*, and *quality*. A fourth property, *duration*, is sometimes included. The number of its vibrations per second determines its pitch as "high" or "low;" the width or amplitude of its vibrations determines its intensity as "loud" or "soft;" the number and strength of its overtones determines its quality or tone color; and the length of time it sounds determines its duration. All tones consist of *both* the *fundamental tone*, or *first partial*, which is produced by the whole elastic or tremulous body, and the series of *partials*, or *overtones*, which are produced by the segments of the vibrating medium. These overtones are in a mathematical ratio to the fundamental tone and are called *harmonics*. Their combination is known as the *harmonic* or *overtone series*, or as the "chord of nature."

# SECTION THREE | Musical Time

Music is a temporal art since time is required for its performance. Today musical time is organized upon our feeling that music has recurrent beats or pulses which can be grouped into equal units of time called *measures*. The duration of tones is related to the beats within a measure. This organization is similar to that of poetry; a *foot* in poetry corresponds to a *measure* in music. Both poetic feet and musical measures result from a series of accented and unaccented syllables or beats. On the other hand, neither prose nor musical chant has regularly recurring spaced accents.

Accents are both physical and psychological in origin, that is, they are produced either by the volume or the length of the tone, or by an imaginary stress such as a listener supplies to the ticking of a clock or the dripping of water. Our response to these two types of accents appears to be instinctive, due possibly to the bodily rhythms of breathing, walking, or heartbeat. Indeed, regular repetition or periodicity pervades all natures. Therefore, it is not strange that our sense of musical time is the motion or flow of music and its most important element.

**1. How is Musical Time organized?**   Musical time is organized in terms of three elements: regular pulsation—*meter;* pitch duration—*rhythm;* and performance speed—*tempo. Meter* deals with the accentual grouping of beats, *rhythm* with the relative length of tones, and *tempo* with the speed at which music is performed.

The term *rhythm* is often used somewhat loosely to describe all three aspects of musical time. Thus, one may say that a performer plays "rhythmically," or that a jazz player "has rhythm," meaning that his sense of musical time is good. Broadly speaking, this meaning of rhythm is acceptable, but the definitions given below should aid you in understanding more precisely the technical organization of musical time.

**2. What is Meter and how is it classified?**   Meter (Gr. *metron,* to measure) is the regular arrangement of accented and unaccented beats. Its basic principle is *periodicity.* Meter provides a constant value for the measurement of the flow of music.

Meter is classified as *duple, triple,* or *quadruple* according to the number of beats within each metric unit or *measure.* Meters are also classified as *simple* or *compound,* depending upon the normal subdivision of the beat into two or three equal parts. (See question 23, Section IV, p. 25.)

**3. What is Rhythm?**   Rhythm (Gr. *rhythmos,* to flow) is the result of durational pitch patterns. The primary factors of rhythm are *emphasis* and *duration.* In contrast to meter, rhythm implies no repetition of a set pattern. In fact, exact repetition often plays little part in rhythm except in certain dances. The emphasis and duration of pitches establish a dynamic rhythmic pattern, which is often more important than the static metric pattern. For example, compare the melodic rhythmic patterns of a waltz with its regular metric accompaniment. The function of rhythm is to establish designs in relation to the metric pattern.

**4. What is Syncopation?**   Syncopation (Gr. *synkope,* cutting up) results from the deliberate dislocation or "cutting up" of either the metric or the rhythmic accents. It is caused by arbitrarily shifting the accent. In other words, it is produced by an artificial accent which contradicts a natural one. It is a crosscurrent in the flow of music. Recall the use of syncopation (indicated by italics) in the following lines from familiar songs:

Weep no more, my la*dy* (My Old Kentucky Home)

'Way down upon de Swanee Riv*er* (Old Folks at Home)

Carry me back to Old Virgin*ny*

Swing *low,* sweet chari*ot*

No*body* knows the trou*ble* I've seen

My bonnie lies over the *ocean*

**5.   What is a Measure?**   A measure is a group of beats forming the basic unit of the meter. *It measures meter visually* by a perpendicular line (a bar) drawn across the staff at the beginning of this basic unit. (See question 11, Section IV, p. 19.) Traditionally, a *measure* is defined as the space between two *bars*. (The measure is often incorrectly called a "bar.") Since music is an aural not a visual art, a measure is best defined as a *pattern of accented and unaccented beats in any order,* but for practical purposes the traditional definition is adequate, provided it is understood to express the *visual* rather than the *aural* content of a measure. (See the opening paragraph of this section, p. 9.)

Often a musical composition does not begin with the first beat of the measure. It may begin with one or more beats which precede the first beat of the first complete measure. These beats are called *upbeats (anacrusis)* because the conductor of a musical ensemble indicates these weaker beats of the measure with an upward motion of his hand. He indicates the *downbeat* (first beat) with a downward hand motion. Usually the value of the upbeat is subtracted from the final measure of the composition. Thus, a song in $\frac{4}{4}$ meter that begins with an upbeat would have only three beats in the last measure. (See example 30, p. 43, example 31, p. 43, and example 35, p. 47.)

**6.   What are the differences between Meter and Rhythm?**   The chief difference between meter and rhythm is that meter is a *constant* division and rhythm is a *variable* division of musical time. In other words, a composition usually has only one metric pattern but many rhythmic patterns. Thus, soldiers march to the meter, not to the rhythm of the music, because their steps coincide with the steady beats (left-right), not with the long and short pitches of the melody.

Other differences between meter and rhythm may be summarized thus:

| METER | RHYTHM |
| --- | --- |
| strict | free |
| repetitive | varied |
| regular | irregular |
| symmetrical | asymmetrical |

Occasionally these characteristics are interchangeable. Thus, certain dance rhythms are almost metrical in their regularity and symmetry. On the other hand, the frequent changes of meter in many contemporary compositions produce irregular and asymmetrical patterns which resemble those of rhythm. (See question 25, Section IV, p. 27.)

Music has always been rhythmical, but it has only been metrical in Western music for a few centuries. Meter has become a stabilizing element in the organization of musical time. Rhythm and meter are interwoven, but they seldom coincide exactly because the duration of tones (rhythm) is usually longer or shorter than the beat (meter). For example, in the tune *America* the rhythm and the meter of the music are identical for the words "My country," but differ for the words "'tis of Thee." In music, meter is the heartbeat and rhythm the flow of the blood stream. They are interactive and reciprocal.

As Stravinsky says, "*Meter* answers the question of how many equal parts the musical unit, which we call a *measure,* is divided into, and *rhythm* answers the question of how these equal parts will be grouped within a given measure."

**7. What is Tempo?**   *Tempo* (Latin, *tempus,* time) is the speed or pace at which music is performed, that is, the speed of its beats. Our sense of tempo may be related to our pulse (72-80 beats per minute) since tempi which differ from it are felt to be fast or slow. Tempo can be indicated precisely by a metronome, a clock-like instrument whose audible ticks representing beats can be adjusted from 40 to 208 per minute. However, tempo is usually indicated approximately by Italian words at the beginning of the composition.

(See the Glossary.) Some composers also use their native language for this purpose. Aesthetically, tempo is always relative since it is influenced by many variable factors. Strictly speaking, tempo does not deal with the organization of musical time but only with its total duration, which varies with individual performers. Thus, the length of a composition varies according to the performer's *tempo* or timing. Essentially tempo is relative and flexible, not absolute and fixed. (See RUBATO in the Glossary. See also question 26, Section IV, p. 27, for the effect of tempo on meter and rhythm.)

## Summary—Musical Time

Our sense of musical time is based upon our feeling for pulse or beat. It is organized in terms of the recurrence, content, and speed of these beats which are called *meter, rhythm,* and *tempo* respectively. These three aspects of musical time are interactive and reciprocal.

1. *Meter* provides a norm for the measurement of musical time. Its basic unit is called a *measure* whose limits are defined in musical notation by perpendicular lines drawn across the staff. Meter is classified in two ways: first, according to the number of beats or pulses contained in each measure as duple, triple, and quadruple; and second, according to the basic subdivision of the beat as simple or compound.

2. *Rhythm* is the pattern resulting from the duration of pitches. Rhythm is variable, but meter is constant; hence their patterns seldom coincide. Rhythmic patterns are often the more important. Meter measures musical time by dividing it into equal units; rhythm organizes these units into varied and meaningful patterns.

3. *Syncopation* is a disturbance of the normal flow of musical time caused by an abnormal metric or rhythmic accent. The effectiveness of syncopation depends upon its conflict with normal accents either previously established or simultaneously heard. Syncopation is accentual distortion.

4. *Tempo* is the pace or speed at which a composition is performed. Tempo is indicated by Italian terms meaning fast, slow, and so forth, or by a marking for the metronome whose ticks can be adjusted to the desired speed of the beats. Tempo is simply the speed of music's flow or current and varies widely according to period, place, and performer.

In conclusion, remember that the three aspects of musical time—meter, rhythm, and tempo—*are actually inherent in the structure of the music* and are independent of any expressive devices such as accent, phrasing, or rubato. In fact, these devices themselves are based upon the structure of the music as truly as are meter, rhythm, and tempo.

# SECTION FOUR | Musical Notation

Like language, music may be written and hence requires an alphabet. However, the writing or notation of music is less precise than that of language because it is impossible to convey adequately by signs or symbols all the subtle nuances of time and tone. At best, the composer can only provide an outline for the performer's guidance.

Early notation was quite vague, but gradually became more precise through the use of better symbols for the location and duration of pitch. Words were added later to describe expressive details of performance, for example, dynamics and tempi. (See the Glossary for definitions of expressive terms in general use.) The symbols used today for the location and the duration of pitches are defined and illustrated below.

# THE LOCATION OF PITCH

Because the piano is easily available, its keyboard is used as a basis for the following explanation of pitch location. Obviously the entire range, or gamut, of the piano keyboard consists of repetitions of a symmetrical pattern of seven white and five black keys arranged thus:

*Example 1.*   The Keyboard Pattern

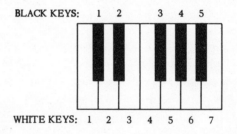

Three basic "tonal spaces" or *intervals* on the piano keyboard should be noted:

1.  A *half step* is the distance between adjacent piano keys, either black or white. The half step is also called a *half tone* or *semitone*. It is the smallest division of pitch commonly used in Western music.

2.  A *whole step* consists of two half steps. The whole step is also called a *whole tone*.

3.  An *octave* (Latin, *octo,* eight) spans eight consecutive white keys of the piano and includes the five intervening black keys. Note that the piano keyboard consists of seven octaves, plus three additional keys, making a total of 88 keys.

**1.  What Alphabet does music use?**   Music uses the first seven letters of our alphabet. The seven basic pitches are represented by any seven white keys of the piano keyboard, beginning with A, the lowest white key at the left, thus:

*Example 2.* The Keyboard Pattern of the Seven Basic Pitches

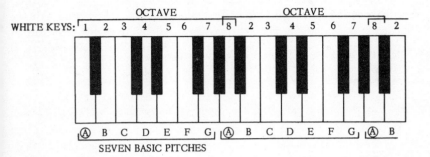

SEVEN BASIC PITCHES

**2. Why are only seven Letters needed?** Only seven letters are needed to represent these pitches because the eighth pitch (white key) duplicates acoustically the first pitch and uses the same letter name. Hence, this series of seven letters may be repeated indefinitely to represent pitch as the seven days of the week are repeated to represent time. The recurrent keyboard pattern illustrates this point. (See example 2 above.)

**3. Is this Alphabet sufficient?** No, seven letters are not sufficient because they provide names for only the white keys of the piano, but not for the five additional black keys whose names are explained in question 6 below.

**4. How many supplementary Symbols are needed?** Five supplementary symbols, called *accidentals*, are needed both to name the black keys on the piano and to indicate a change of pitch without a change of letter. The names, symbols, and effects of the accidentals are as follows:

| NAME | SYMBOL | | EFFECT |
|------|--------|--|--------|
| sharp | ♯ | ⎫ | one half step higher |
| flat | ♭ | | one half step lower |
| double sharp | × | indicates the pitch | one whole step higher |
| double flat | ♭♭ | ⎭ | one whole step lower |
| natural | ♮ | ⎬ | cancels any of the above *accidentals* |

Thus the term C-sharp (C♯) refers to the pitch one half tone above C, namely the adjacent black key to the right. (The term *accidental* is used in several senses. For further discussion, see KEY SIGNATURES, questions 25-27, Section V, p. 44.)

**5. How are these supplementary Symbols used?**  These supplementary symbols of pitch inflection are used in three ways:

A.   To provide names for the five additional "black-key" pitches within the octave.

B.   To provide a means for expressing *enharmonic notation*. (See questions 9 and 10 below.)

C.   To provide means for expressing certain tonal relationships. (See question 4, Section VI, p. 58.)

*Accidentals* operate only within their own measure unless grouped in a *key signature*. (*See* KEY SIGNATURES, questions 25-27, Section V, p. 44.)

**6. How are Black Keys named?**  Black keys are named by using the letter-name of either one of their two adjacent white keys plus a supplementary sharp or flat, for example, C♯ or D♭.

**7. Why do Black Keys have two names?**  Black keys have two names because of their dual relationship to their adjacent white keys. The name depends upon this *relationship* and is changed when the relationship changes.

**8. How is the name of a Black Key chosen and what does it show?**  The name of a black key is chosen to show its *relationship* to its adjacent white keys. Thus, the black key between A and B is named either A-sharp (A♯) or B-flat (B♭) depending upon its temporary relationship to one of these tones.

*Example 3.*    Relationships of the Black and White Piano Keys

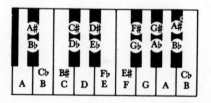

**9. What is Enharmonic Notation?** *Enharmonic notation* is the possible use of two or more different names for the same pitch. As shown in example 3 above, the pitch of each black key can be written in two ways, that is, *enharmonically*. The same principle also applies to white keys, especially where there is no intervening black key, as B-C and E-F. Here the complex relationships discussed in question 4, Section VI, p. 58, may demand the following enharmonic notations:

| | | | |
|---|---|---|---|
| C♭ | for B | F♭ | for E |
| B♯ | for C | E♯ | for F |

Similarly B may be written also as A✕ . Thus, any white key may have three different names.

**10. Why is Enharmonic Notation necessary?** Primarily, enharmonic notation is necessary because music is written according to its *tonal relationships* ("meanings") rather than according to its *sound*. In this respect, music is like language in which the same sound or word is spelled differently according to its context or meaning, for example, *to, too,* and *two.*

**11. How are Pitches represented and located?** Pitches are represented on paper by *notes* written upon a *staff* (plural, *staves*). The staff consists of five parallel, equidistant, horizontal lines and four intervening spaces to which are assigned definite pitches in alphabetical order upward from the bottom of the staff.

Pitches are located on the staff by a symbol called a *clef* (Latin, *clavis,* key) which fixes the position of one letter or pitch as a point of reference for all other pitches on the staff.

**12. How many Staves are used?** The number of staves used in writing music varies according to the instruments and voices as follows:

A.   pipe organ—three staves
B.   other keyboard instruments and harp—two staves
C.   each orchestral instrument or vocal part—one staff
D.   orchestral instruments of indefinite pitch—no staff

(See A Classification of Instruments, Section VIII, p. 86.)

**13.   What is a group of Staves called?**   A group of staves used for notating chamber, choral, or orchestral music is called a *score*. There are three types of scores:

A.   A *full* score gives each instrumental and vocal line on a separate staff.

B.   A *vocal* score gives each vocal part on a separate line but reduces the orchestral accompaniment to an arrangement for piano on two staves.

C.   A *short (piano)* score gives the reduction of either the instrumental or vocal parts on two staves for convenient reading.

(Note: The combination of staves used solely for keyboard instruments or the harp is not called a score.)

**14.   How many Clefs are used?**   Three clefs are used:

A.   The F, or *bass* clef, centered upon the fourth line of the staff.

B.   The C, or *alto-tenor* clef, centered upon the third or fourth lines respectively.

C.   The G or *treble* clef, centered upon the second line.

*Example 4.*   The Clefs

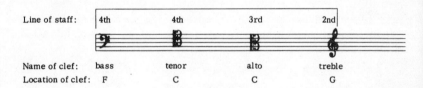

| Line of staff: | 4th | 4th | 3rd | 2nd |
|---|---|---|---|---|
| Name of clef: | bass | tenor | alto | treble |
| Location of clef: | F | C | C | G |

**15.   How are these Clefs used?**   The F, C, and G clefs are used for pitches in low, middle, and high registers respectively, as represented by the bass, tenor or alto, and soprano voices. The F and G clefs are used most frequently for both vocal and instrumental music. Formerly the C clef was used more widely, but today its use is restricted to music written for certain orchestral instruments, such as the viola. The pitch C, common to all three clefs, is called *middle* C since it is in the middle of the vocal compass. All voices from low bass to high soprano can sing this pitch. The G and F clefs locate pitches of those names which are immediately above and below middle C respectively, thus:

*Example 5.*    The Range of the Clefs

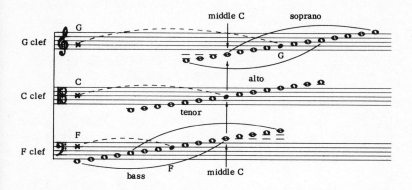

Note that the compass of all the staves may be extended by short supplementary lines above or below the staff. These additional lines are called *leger* (or *ledger*) lines. The origin of the leger line is explained in the following question.

**16.  What is the Great Staff?**   The *great staff* is a combination of two staves usually employing the F and G clefs. Its most familiar example is music written for piano in which the lower staff (using the F clef) is played by the left hand and the upper staff (using the G clef) by the right hand.

Originally the great staff was one large eleven-line staff.

*Example 6.*    The Original Great Staff

To facilitate reading, this eleven-line staff was later subdivided into two groups of five lines each, the eleventh line in the center being reduced to a short line between the two staves called a *leger* (or *ledger*) line representing *middle* C. This leger line is printed only when needed.

*Example 7.*   The Modern Staves

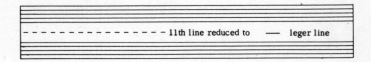

**17.   How may the Compass of the Staves be extended?**   The compass of any staff may be extended by adding the required number of *leger* lines above or below it. If the number of *leger* lines becomes excessive, it can be reduced by using the abbreviations, *8ᵛᵃ* or *8ᵛᵃ bassa,* meaning that the notes are to be played on octave higher or lower respectively than written, thus:

*Example 8.*   Extension of the Compass of the Staves

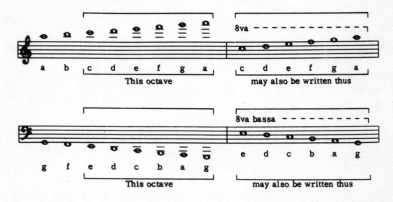

# THE DURATION OF PITCH

**18.   How is the Duration of Pitches indicated?**   The duration as well as the location of pitches is indicated by *notes* written differently to represent different time values. The note values in use today, with their equivalent *rests* for periods of silence, are as follows:

| VALUE | NOTE | REST |
|-------|------|------|
| whole | o | ▬ |
| half | ♩ | ▬ |
| quarter | ♩ | ⸒ |
| eighth | ♪ | 𝄿 |
| sixteenth | ♬ | 𝄾 |
| thirty-second | ♬ | 𝄿 |
| sixty-fourth | ♬ | 𝄿 |

Note values of shorter duration than a quarter note may be joined by a line called a *beam*, thus:

$$\sqcap = ♪♪ \quad \text{or} \quad \overline{♬♬} = ♪♪♪♪$$

When the whole note is accepted as the unit for measuring the relative duration of musical tones, all the other note values are proportional. For example, the half note becomes one half of the whole note.

**19. Can these Time Values be modified?**    Yes, usually time values are modified in two ways:

A. by the use of one or more *dots* placed after the note or rest.
B. by the use of a *tie*, a curved line joining two or more notes of the same pitch only the first of which is sounded. Rest values can be modified only by the dot, not by the tie.

Exceptionally, time values may be either shortened or lengthened by a group of notes or rests which do not conform to the prevailing type of subdivision or multiplication. These irregular patterns usually shorten time values, the most familiar being three eighth notes

performed in the time of two, written 𝅘𝅥𝅮𝅘𝅥𝅮𝅘𝅥𝅮 = 𝅘𝅥𝅮𝅘𝅥𝅮 and called a
                                                3

*triplet*. Note that the exceptional division of the beat is indicated
by the number 3. However, the reverse is also true; time values may
be lengthened when fewer notes or rests are used than a unit nor-
mally requires. Hence, if two eighth notes are to be performed in the
time of three, they would be written 𝅘𝅥𝅮𝅘𝅥𝅮 = 𝅘𝅥𝅮𝅘𝅥𝅮𝅘𝅥𝅮 and called a *duplet*.
                                                        2

Many such irregular groupings occur in even simple music. In
all cases the exceptional subdivision of the beat is always shown by
an arabic number written either above or below the irregular group.

*Example 9.*    Exceptional Subdivisions of Beats. All these exceptional sub-
                divisions occur in Chopin, "Nocturne in F♯ Major,"
                op. 9, no. 3.

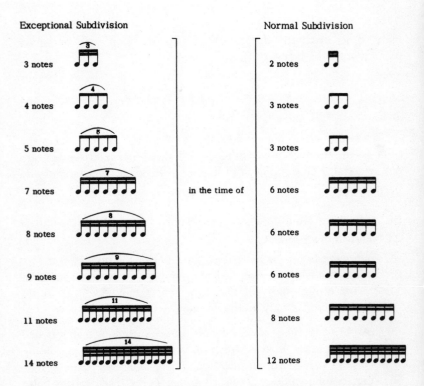

**20. How do Dots affect Time Values?** A *dot* increases the value of a note by one half, and additional dots increase the value proportionately. A single dot increases a half note by one quarter note, two dots by a quarter plus an eighth note, and three dots by a quarter and an eighth plus a sixteenth note. The use of more than two dots is extremely rare. The value of rests may be similarly increased. Today, dots operate only within a measure; across a bar it is necessary to use a tie.

*Example 10.* Use of the Tie

**21. What is a Time Signature?** A *time* or *metric* signature consists of two numbers written vertically at the beginning of a composition to indicate its meter and unit of rhythm. The upper number denotes the meter, that is, the number of beats or pulses in a measure. The lower number denotes the unit of rhythm, that is, the note value equivalent to the beat. Thus, the time signature $\frac{3}{4}$ means that each measure of the composition will contain three beats, each beat being represented by a quarter note or its equivalent. In other words, $\frac{3}{4}$ means

$$\frac{\text{number of beats}}{\text{value of one beat}} \quad \text{or roughly} \quad \frac{\text{meter}}{\text{rhythm}}.$$

Hence, a time signature shows the temporal content of each measure in terms of its metric pattern and rhythmic unit.

**22. How many Time Signatures are used?** Theoretically, the number of possible time signatures is large, eighteen or more, but practically, the number is limited to the signatures listed in example 11 below. Each time signature in this example is repeated in parentheses giving the unit of rhythm in note values rather than by number. Thus, $\frac{2}{4}$ means $\frac{2}{\eighthnote}$ , that is, two quarter notes (or equivalents) in each measure |♩ ♩|. The symbol $\frac{2}{4}$ is pronounced "two-four."

**23. How are Time Signatures classified?** Time signatures are classified in two ways: *metrically* as duple, triple, or quadruple according to the number of beats represented; and *rhythmically* as simple or compound according to the basic subdivision of the beat. If the basic subdivision of the beat is in two or its multiples, the meter is *simple;* if in three, it is *compound.* In the latter case, the unit of rhythm will be a dotted note, for example, ♩. or ♪. .

*Example 11.*    Time Signatures. For a definition of *alla breve,* see the Glossary.

Simple

> Duple: $\frac{2}{4}$ ($\frac{2}{♩}$); $\frac{2}{2}$ ($\frac{2}{♩}$), also written ¢ and called *alla breve*. (Often incorrectly called "cut time.")
>
> Triple: $\frac{3}{8}$ ($\frac{3}{♪}$); $\frac{3}{4}$ ($\frac{3}{♩}$); $\frac{3}{2}$ ($\frac{3}{♩}$)
>
> Quadruple: $\frac{4}{8}$ ($\frac{4}{♪}$); $\frac{4}{4}$ ($\frac{4}{♩}$), also written C; $\frac{4}{2}$ ($\frac{4}{♩}$). (Often incorrectly called "common time.")

Compound

> Duple: $\frac{6}{8}$ ($\frac{2}{♩.}$), $\frac{6}{4}$ ($\frac{2}{♩.}$)
>
> Triple: $\frac{9}{8}$ ($\frac{3}{♩.}$), $\frac{9}{4}$ ($\frac{3}{♩.}$)
>
> Quadruple: $\frac{12}{8}$ ($\frac{4}{♩.}$)

**24.    Are additional Time Signatures needed?**    Yes, a few additional time signatures are needed to express unusual combinations of meters, for example $\frac{5}{4}$ which is actually $\frac{3}{4} + \frac{2}{4}$ or $\frac{2}{4} + \frac{3}{4}$ as shown in the following example:

*Example 12.*    The Use of an Additional Time Signature. (The original key is D major.)

**25. How do contemporary composers treat Meter and Rhythm?**
Contemporary composers treat both meter and rhythm freely. As
regards meter, time signatures often change frequently, thus:

*Example 13.*    The Free Use of Meter

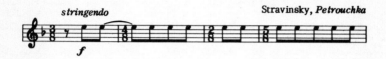

As regards rhythm, freedom is achieved either by exceptional grouping of note values within a measure, or by the abolition of the
measure (and hence of the time signature) which produces a free
rhythm similar to that of the Gregorian chant, thus:

*Example 14.*    The Free Use of Rhythm

**26. Does Tempo affect Meter and Rhythm?**    Yes, *tempo* does
affect both meter and rhythm. In fact, tempo (or the speed of the
beats) determines to a large extent how much we hear in music, just
as our speed in traveling by car or train determines how much we
see. When the musical speed or tempo is slow, we hear more; when
rapid, we hear less. Both speeds have their advantages—one empha-
sizes details, the other generalities.

In a broad sense, tempo (not the time signature) determines the
unit of rhythm, that is, it determines what is heard as one pulse.

Compound meters, when played rapidly, sound like simple meters, $\frac{6}{8}$ in a rapid tempo is heard as having only two (not six) beats in a measure, the value of each beat being a dotted quarter note. The songs "Row, Row, Row Your Boat" and "The Kerry Dance" are written in $\frac{6}{8}$, but are heard as having two beats per measure. On the other hand, in songs of slower tempo such as "Drink to Me Only" and "Silent Night," also notated in $\frac{6}{8}$, six beats per measure may be heard.

The same principle applies to simple meters performed rapidly in which a whole measure on paper is reduced to a single beat by the ear. In other words, a *visual measure* becomes an *aural beat,* as in the Beethoven *scherzi* and other music in a very fast tempo, thus:

*Example 15.*    Visual Measures that Become Aural Beats

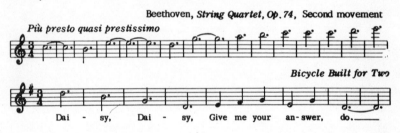

Conversely, a slow tempo tends to subdivide the beat aurally, thereby producing more accents within the measure, thus:

*Example 16.*    Aural subdivisions of Visual Beats

Tempo also affects rhythm since meter and rhythm are the Siamese twins of musical time and are interactive. The most obvious effect of speed upon rhythm is *tempo rubato* (It., robbed), meaning an elasticity of performance within the beat, measure, or phrase.

**27. Are Tempi and Note values related?** This question can be answered only in terms of value and duration, that is, the dual relationship of note values to each other and to tempi. In regard to each other, notes do have a fixed and absolute time value, that is, a whole note is four times as long as a quarter note *in the same tempo.* In relation to different tempi, however, these fixed or absolute note values disappear. For example, a whole note played in a very fast tempo of course would be shorter in *duration* than a quarter note played in a very slow tempo. In other words, fixed note values are valid only in the same tempo; different tempi result in different, changing values. Mathematical note values are fixed, but durational values vary.

Thus, fast music is not necessarily expressed by small note values, nor must slow music be written in large note values. The choice rests with the composer who may be influenced by whim, custom, or historical precedent. This means that the same music written in $\frac{3}{8}$ and $\frac{3}{2}$ sounds precisely alike *if the tempo is the same.* Music in $\frac{3}{8}$ is not faster than that in $\frac{3}{2}$ unless its indicated *tempo* is faster. For example, these three versions of "America" (sung at the same speed) are identical in sound.

*Example 17.* The Same Music Written with Different Time Signatures

**28. Why is Musical Notation inaccurate?**  Musical notation, as a printed or written guide for performance, is inaccurate primarily because it is necessarily visual, whereas music is an aural not a visual art and cannot be written precisely. Hence, what is heard does not always agree with what is seen. Furthermore, each performance differs from the printed music, not only because of different interpretations, but also because of the influence of tradition and the composer's indifference or ignorance regarding clear and logical notation.

## Summary—Musical Notation

Musical notation shows both the *location* of pitches in musical space, as "high" or "low," and their *duration* in musical time, as "long" or "short."

1. *The location of musical tones* is illustrated by the piano keyboard. The distance between adjacent keys is called a *half step, half tone,* or *semitone.* A *whole step,* or *whole tone,* consists of two half steps. An *octave* consists of eight consecutive white keys or of thirteen consecutive keys of both colors. The outer tones of an octave are equivalent acoustically. The octave is the unit of pitch measurement and the basis of the piano's recurrent keyboard pattern.

Because of the octave relationship, only the first seven letters of our alphabet are needed to name the white keys on the piano. To name the black keys and to express complex tonal relationships, a series of five supplementary symbols called *accidentals* are required. These symbols are single and double *sharps* and *flats,* and the *natural.* The single sharps and flats indicate pitches one half-step higher and lower respectively than the letter which they modify. *Double sharps* and *flats* alter the pitch one whole step, and the *natural* cancels the effect of any other accidental. These symbols operate only within their own measure unless they are part of a key signature. (See KEY SIGNATURE, question 25, Section V, p. 44.)

A black key is named from its relationship to either of its two adjacent white keys. This duality of spelling (different names for the same pitch) is called *enharmonic* notation and is necessary for the expression of complex tonal relationships.

Pitches are represented on paper by *notes* written upon five parallel, equidistant, horizontal lines and four spaces called a *staff* (pl., *staves*). Each successive line and space is named in alphabetical order until the eighth degree is reached, which is a duplicate acoustically of the first and uses the same letter name. These eight degrees constitute an *octave.* The number of staves used depends upon the medium of performance. The *great staff* is a combination of two staves used especially for piano music. A *score* is the group of staves used for notating chamber, choral, or orchestral music. The compass of the staff may be extended by adding short additional *leger* (*ledger*) lines above or below it, by using the abbreviation 8$^{va}$, or by both.

The location of pitches on the staff is determined by a *clef* which fixes the pitch corresponding to its name. There are three clefs in use: the G (treble), the F (bass), and the C (alto or tenor) clefs, the latter being used today only for certain orchestral instruments. The G and F clefs are centered on the second and fourth staff lines respectively; the C clef is centered on either the third or fourth line, depending upon the instrument. In vocal music the G and F clefs are used for treble and bass voices respectively; in piano music, for the right and left hands respectively.

2. *The duration of pitches* is represented by notes of different time values with their equivalent *rests* for silence. Note values are based essentially upon the division of a *whole note* into two or its multiples. Other values are obtained by adding *dots*, which increase the value of the note or rest proportionately, or by a *tie* (curved line) joining two notes representing the same pitch, the second of which is not sounded. Irregular divisions of the beat are indicated by an Arabic numeral above or below a group of notes.

A *time* or *metric signature* consists of two vertical numbers, the upper denoting the meter and the lower the unit of rhythm. Time signatures are classified metrically as duple, triple, or quadruple, and rhythmically as simple or compound. About a dozen time signatures are in general use, the most frequent being $\frac{2}{2}$ ($\mathcal{C}$), $\frac{2}{4}$, $\frac{3}{4}$, $\frac{4}{4}$ (C), and $\frac{6}{8}$. Theoretically eighteen or more time signatures are possible.

Two meters sometimes occur consecutively within a measure and are often represented by a single time signature, for example, $\frac{5}{4}$ which is equivalent to $\frac{3}{4}$ plus $\frac{2}{4}$ or $\frac{2}{4}$ plus $\frac{3}{4}$. Contemporary treatment of both rhythm and meter is quite free and may include frequent changes of meter, exceptional subdivisions of the measure, and simultaneous combinations of complex rhythms and meters in different parts or voices.

*Tempo* vitally affects both meter and rhythm since it determines aurally the true meter and rhythmic unit as opposed to the visual one of the time signature. Rhythm is chiefly affected by *tempo rubato*, a free, flexible performance of the contents of the beat, measure, or phrase. In theory, aural and visual impressions of musical time should agree, but in practice they often differ, partly because performers' interpretations of music differ, but chiefly because the subtleties of music defy precise notation. As Haydn said, "the ear, not the eye, is the sole judge of music."

# SECTION FIVE

# Musical Relationships —Single Tones

The raw material of music is tone, which is organized for expressive purposes in terms of time and pitch. The principal elements in the organization of music are *rhythm,* dealing with musical time, and *melody* and *harmony,* which are concerned with pitches. These are the three structural elements of music. A composer uses them to express his musical ideas. The sequence of these ideas is called *form,* corresponding to the plot of a story or the design of a building.

The nature of musical time has been discussed in Section III. Sections V, VI, and VII will deal primarily with tonal relationships of melody and of harmony and how they are used in simple musical forms. Definitions of melodic and harmonic relationships depend upon the concept of *tonality,* including keys, scales, and modes, which we shall presently examine.

It should be noted that definition of these musical relationships is hampered by semantic difficulties. Many of the terms overlap in content and hence are difficult to define precisely. There is little agreement among authorities regarding certain areas of meaning. Possibly consistency is the most that can be achieved in the following definitions.

**1. How are Tones related?**    Tones are related in two ways—physically and expressively.

**A.** Physical relationships are based upon the natural laws of acoustics. All harmonics or overtones are related to their fundamental tone because they are derived from it. This acoustical fact has been used to explain many musical relationships, chiefly *the supremacy of one tone in a group of related tones,* which is universal except in the "atonal" music of the twentieth century. (See ATONAL-ITY in the Glossary.)

**B.** Expressive relationships are based upon both natural law and instinctive musical feeling which later may be found to have a rational basis. Expressive relationships usually are influenced by psychological and aesthetic factors beyond the scope of the discussion in this book. "Atonal" music is a good example of purely expressive relationships.

There is little agreement regarding the relative importance of physical versus expressive relationships. Certainly they are interactive. Music is both a science and an art, both physical and psychological, but the relationship of these dual aspects is obscure.

**2. What Tonal relationships are illustrated by the Piano Keyboard?**
The four tonal relationships or patterns of Western music illustrated by the piano keyboard are:

**A.** diatonic—the white keys only (seven tones)
**B.** pentatonic—the black keys only (five tones)
**C.** chromatic—the black and white keys consecutively (twelve tones)
**D.** whole-tone—the combination of black and white keys each separated by one intervening key (six tones)

*Example 18.*   The Four Tonal Relationships of Western Music

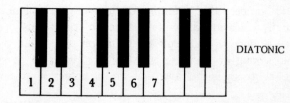

DIATONIC

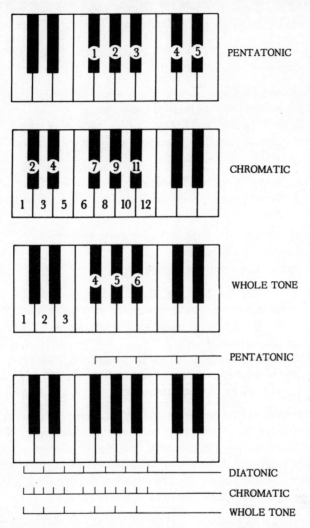

3. **What are groups of related single Tones called?** Groups of related single tones are called scales, modes, keys, tonalities, and melodies according to their functions.

4. **What is a Scale?** A scale (It., *scala*, ladder) is the tonal material of music arranged in consecutive pitch order. Obviously this material varies so widely according to time and place that a great number of scales exist.

**5. What types of Scales do we use?**   Four types of scales are generally used in Western music: the diatonic, pentatonic, chromatic and whole-tone scales, as illustrated by the piano keyboard in example 18 above. All these types can be derived from the diatonic scales used by the ancient Greeks.

**6. What are Diatonic Scales?**   The word *diatonic* is derived from two Greek words: *dia,* through, and *tonos,* a tone, meaning to pass through all tones. Diatonic scales consist of the first seven letters in alphabetical order beginning with any letter, as illustrated by the white keys of the piano.

**7. How many types of Diatonic Scales exist?**   There are three types of diatonic scales, each illustrated by seven white keys of the piano, thus:

**A.**  a modal scale—beginning on any white key
**B.**  a major scale—beginning on C
**C.**  a minor scale—beginning on A

**8. What is a Modal Scale or Mode?**   The word *mode* is derived from the Latin *modus,* meaning measure, rhythm, meter, manner, or form. Hence, in medieval music the term was used for both pitch and rhythmic patterns.

Historically, the medieval modes concerned with pitch patterns were the chief bases of Western music before 1600. They were derived from Greek and Oriental sources.

**9. How are Modal Scales named?**   The general names for modal scales used by the Roman Catholic church came from the Gregorian chant (plain song or plain chant). Specifically, they were numbered Mode I, or Tone I; Mode II, or Tone II; and so forth. The medieval modes were also known by a series of titles borrowed, rather inaccurately, from the ancient Greek modes as follows:

| | | |
|---|---|---|
| Dorian: | d e f g a b c d | ⎫ |
| Phrygian: | e f g a b c d e | ⎪ |
| Lydian: | f g a b c d e f | ⎬  Church modes |
| Mixolydian: | g a b c d e f g | ⎭ |

| | | |
|---|---|---|
| Aeolian: | a b c d e f g a   —natural minor scale | ⎫ |
| Locrian:* | b c d e f g a b | ⎬ Secular modes |
| Ionian: | c d e f g a b c—major scale | ⎭ |

\* Because its intervals were objectionable to medieval theorists, the Locrian mode was artificial and was not used.

Each mode had both an *authentic* and a plagal form, depending upon its melodic range used. The prefix *hypo* indicated the plagal form thus:

| | |
|---|---|
| Hypodorian: | a b **c** d e f g a |
| Hypophrygian: | b c **d** e f g a b |
| Hypolydian: | c d **e** f g a b c |
| Hypomixolydian: | d e **f** g a b c d |
| Hypoaeolian: | e f **g** a b c d e |
| Hypolocrian: | f g **a** b c d e f |
| Hypoionian: | g a **b** c d e f g |

**Bold-letter** tones indicate the *finalis*, or center tone.

The *plagal* modes had the same *finalis* as their corresponding *authentic* forms. In the plagal forms, however, the finalis appeared in the middle rather than the extremes of their ranges. For details regarding the medieval modes, consult any standard reference work.

**10. How are Modal Scales used?** Today the modal scales are used in three ways:

**A.** as our major and minor scales (Ionian and Aeolian modes respectively)
**B.** as the basis for much folk music
**C.** as means for obtaining special harmonic and melodic effects

**11. What is a Major Scale?** A major scale is a pattern consisting of whole and half steps, the half steps occurring between the third and fourth degrees and between the seventh and eighth degrees. Its pattern coincides with the Ionian mode and hence with the white keys of the piano beginning on C. The scale names and pitches are as follows:

*Example 19.* The Major Scale Pattern

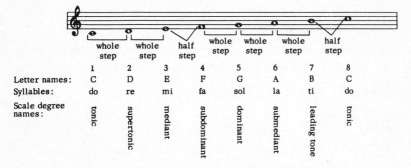

| | whole step | whole step | half step | whole step | whole step | whole step | half step | |
|---|---|---|---|---|---|---|---|---|
| | 1 | 2 | 3 | 4 | 5 | 6 | 7 | 8 |
| Letter names: | C | D | E | F | G | A | B | C |
| Syllables: | do | re | mi | fa | sol | la | ti | do |
| Scale degree names: | tonic | supertonic | mediant | subdominant | dominant | submediant | leading tone | tonic |

**12. What is a Minor Scale?** Historically, the minor scale pattern coincides with the Aeolian mode and with the white keys of the piano beginning on A.

*Example 20.* A Minor Scale Pattern

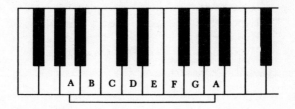

Logically, a minor scale is a major scale whose third step (mediant) is lowered one half tone. Thus, there are two explanations of the minor scale pattern: *traditionally,* the minor scale is derived from the Aeolian mode, but *aurally,* it sounds like the major scale having a lowered mediant. Endless confusion and considerable heat have been generated by these divergent views. However, since music is an aural art, the second theory seems preferable.

**13. How many Forms of the Minor Scale exist?** There are three forms of the minor scale: the *harmonic, melodic,* and *natural.* The latter is called also the *pure* or *Aeolian* minor scale because of its derivation from the Aeolian mode. (See example 20 above.) As their names indicate, the first two forms are necessary for harmonic and melodic reasons. The third form, the Aeolian, is found in folk music and is often used in art music for modal effects.

**14. How are these Forms constructed?** The three forms of the minor scale are best constructed as variants of the major scale beginning on the same pitch:

**A.** *The harmonic minor scale,* by lowering one half step the third and sixth degrees of the corresponding major scale.

*Example 21.* The Harmonic Minor Scale

**B.** *The melodic minor scale,* by lowering the third degree ascending and the seventh, sixth, and third degrees descending of the corresponding major scale.

*Example 22.*   The Melodic Minor Scale

**C.** *The natural minor scale* (pure or Aeolian minor), uses the pattern of the descending melodic minor scale in both directions.

*Example 23.*   The Natural Minor Scale

Note that no mention has been made regarding the location of the whole and half steps in these variants of the minor scale. Such a method is complex and confusing. The same objection can be made to the use of *tetrachords* in constructing minor scales. (See TETRACHORD in the Glossary.)

**15.   How are these Forms used?** The use of these forms of the minor scale is determined by a number of complex harmonic and melodic factors which may be summarized thus:

**A.** *The harmonic minor* scale is used chiefly for building chords and in melodies when the sixth and seventh scale degrees do not occur consecutively.

*Example 24.*   The Harmonic Minor Scale Used in a Melody. The asterisks indicate chromatic tones. See question 23, p. 43.

**B.** *The melodic minor scale* is used whenever the sixth and
seventh scale degrees occur consecutively, that is, for the scale progressions 6-7 or 7-6. The choice of the ascending or descending form
depends upon the implied harmonic background of the sixth and
seventh degrees, *not* upon the direction of the direction of the
melody.

*Example 25.*   The Melodic Minor Scale Used in a Melody

**C.** The *natural minor scale* is used chiefly for modal effects. If
used as a basis for chords, its effect is archaic. It is often found in
modal melodies.

*Example 26.*   The Natural Minor Scale Used in a Modal Melody

**16. What is a Pentatonic Scale?** A pentatonic scale is a primitive scale consisting of only five consecutive tones within the octave. Theoretically, there are an infinite number of such scales. Practically, the one found most often corresponds to the black keys of the piano, beginning on any one of them, thus:

*Example 27.* A Pentatonic Scale

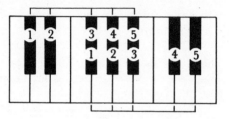

**17. What is a Whole-tone Scale?** A whole-tone scale consists entirely of whole steps, thus having only six consecutive tones within the octave. Its pattern is reproduced by playing alternate piano keys of both colors beginning on any pitch.

*Example 28.* A Whole-tone Scale

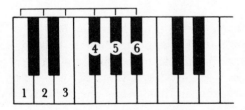

The notation of a whole-tone scale is arbitrary, and its effect on tonality vague. (See question 35 below. For an interesting example of a composition constructed entirely of the whole-tone and pentatonic scales, see the Debussy *Preludes*, Book I, No. 2.)

**18. What is the Chromatic Scale?** The chromatic scale (Gr., *chroma,* color) consists of twelve pitches within an octave in consecutive order, the pitches of all the black and white piano keys. The chromatic scale is seldom used in its entirety. In general, chromaticism was little used before 1600. Its use increased in the eighteenth century and became extensive in the nineteenth and twentieth centuries.

**19. How is the Chromatic Scale written?** The complete chromatic scale is written in terms of the key and mode in which it occurs. In the key of C major it is written:

*Example 29.* The Chromatic Scale in the Key of C Major. See question 33, p. 49 for the reason why F♯ is used descending rather than G♭.

C C♯ D D♯ E F F♯ G G♯ A A♯ B C B B♭ A A♭ G F♯ F E E♭ D D♭ C

**20. What is a Key?** The term *key* is one of the most ambiguous terms in music. It refers both to the finger mechanism used in playing instruments and also to a group of related tones similar to a scale. Hence, there are major and minor keys as well as scales.

**21. How are the Tones of a Major Key related?** The tones of a major key are related acoustically because they can be arranged in the simplest mathematical ratio, namely a series of perfect fifths. (See questions 2 and 4, Section VI, p. 57). When arranged in fifths, that is, five letters apart, the tones of the key of C major are:

F   C   G   D   A   E   B

The generating tone is called the *key tone,* which is equivalent to the *tonic* of the scale.

**22. How are Keys and Scales similar?** Keys and scales are similar because they consist basically of the same tones arranged differently. (See question 21 above.)

**23.  How do Keys and Scales differ?**   Keys and scales differ in both the order and number of tones which they contain. The key includes more tonal material than the scale, for example, chromatic tones (or chords) which are foreign to the scale but included in the key. Thus a melody in the key of C major could contain embellishing chromatic tones and yet remain in that key, although these tones would be outside the scale. Note the chromatic tone marked with an asterisk (*) in the melody of "America, the Beautiful":

*Example 30.*   A Chromatic Tone in a Melody in C Major

Note the more frequent use of chromatic tones in the first two phrases of the song "Sweet Genevieve":

*Example 31.*   Frequent Use of Chromatic Tones in a Melody

Thus, a composition is said to be in a particular key rather than a scale, because the term *key* is a broader and more inclusive term than *scale*.

**24.  How many Major and Minor Scales are there?**   Aurally there are twenty-four scales, twelve major and twelve minor, beginning on each of the twelve pitches in the octave. However, a total of thirty major and minor scales may be written since three of each may be written enharmonically.

**25. What is a Key Signature?** A key signature is the group of sharps or flats at the beginning of each staff which indicates the key of the composition. Since C major (and the natural form of A minor) are the only scales consisting entirely of white keys on the piano, obviously scales beginning on other pitches must include some black keys whose notation requires additional symbols known as *accidentals*. Actually, the purpose of the key signature is to maintain the same scale pattern irrespective of the tone on which the scale begins. A key signature simply saves the composer the trouble of writing all the necessary accidentals as they occur in scales other than the C major and A minor scales.

A key signature indicates that the pitches be altered accordingly whenever they occur unless canceled by another accidental.

*Example 32.*    Alteration of Pitches. (a) Using accidentals. (b) Using a key signature.

**26. How many Key Signatures are required?** Only fourteen key signatures are required because major and minor keys share the same signatures. Key signatures are constructed only for major keys. The minor keys "borrow" their signatures from related major keys. (See question 32 below.) Chromatic scales use the key signature of the prevailing tonality. Seven "sharp" (♯) and seven "flat" (♭) key signatures are required, making a total of fourteen although there are only twelve pitches in the octave. This is because some keys may be written two ways, that is, enharmonically. Theoretically, all keys could be written enharmonically, but the practical limit is three keys of each mode.

**27. What are the names of the Major Key Signatures?** The major key signatures used, arranged consecutively, are as follows:

*Example 33.*  Major Key Signatures Using Sharp Signatures and Flat Signatures

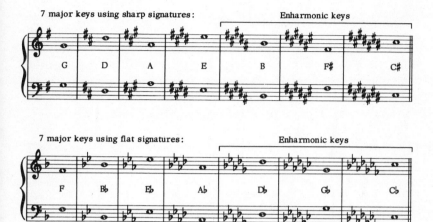

Three additional points regarding these key signatures should be mentioned:

**A.** Each accidental in the signature is placed to the right of the one preceeding it in a definite position on the staff. The signature is effective in all registers throughout the composition unless temporarily cancelled by an additional accidental on the staff or by a change of key signature.

**B.** Keys are related by perfect fifths as are the tones in a key.

**C.** The last three sharp scales (B, F♯, and C♯) may be written enharmonically as C♭, G♭, and D♭ respectively.

**28.  How are Major Key Signatures recognized?**  Major key signatures may be recognized by locating the *tonic* of their scales (and hence their *keytone*), thus:

**A.** Sharp keys—the tonic is the letter one half step above the last sharp.

**B.** Flat keys—the tonic is the same as the next to the last flat.

**29. What is the Circle of Keys?**   The circle of keys is the clockwise rather than the vertical diagram of keys, thus:

*Example 34.*   The Circle of Major Keys

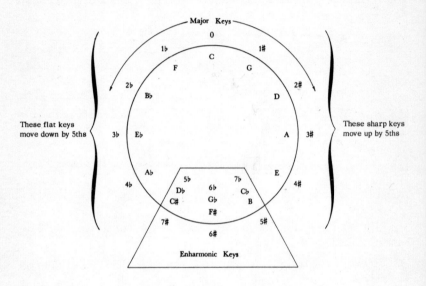

The number of the letter counting both left and right from C corresponds to the accidentals required by that key—for example, G is one ♯ , and F is one ♭ .

**30. What Signatures do the Minor Keys use?**   The minor keys "borrow" the major signatures which best fit their structure. The essential difference between major and minor scales is the lowered third step of the minor scale in contrast with the major scale. The signature of this lowered third step is "borrowed" for the minor scale and for its key, as shown by the following familiar song "Go Down, Moses."

*Example 35.* Signature Borrowed by a Minor Scale. (a) Lowered 3rd step (B♭ ) written with accidentals. (b) Lowered 3rd step (B♭ ) written with B♭ signature.

*a)* G minor
(signature of G major)

| | When | Is-rael | was | in | E-gypt's | land: | Let | my | peo-ple | go, |
|---|---|---|---|---|---|---|---|---|---|---|
| Scale steps | 5 | 3 | 3 | 2 | 2 | 3 | 3 | 1 | 5 5 7 7 | 8 |
| Pitches | D | B♭ | B♭ | A | A | B♭ | B♭ | G | D D F♯ F♯ | G |

*b)* G minor
(borrowed signature of
B♭ major)

**31. What are the Names and Signatures of the Minor Keys?** The following are the signatures used for minor keys arranged in consecutive order:

*Example 36.* Minor Key Signatures Using Sharp Signatures and Flat Signatures

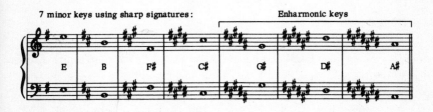

7 minor keys using sharp signatures:            Enharmonic keys

E    B    F♯    C♯    G♯    D♯    A♯

7 minor keys using flat signatures:            Enharmonic keys

D    G    C    F    B♭    E♭    A♭

Note that the last three sharp scales (G♯, D♯, and A♯) may be written enharmonically as A♭, E♭, and B♭ respectively.

Arranged in a circle of fifths, the minor keys appear as follows:

*Example 37.*   The Circle of Minor Keys

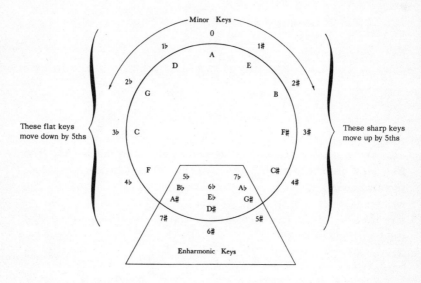

**32.   What are Parallel and Relative Scales?**   *Parallel* major and minor scales have the same key tone or tonic and the same name—G major and G minor. *Relative* major and minor scales use the same key signature—B-flat major and G minor. Since parallel major and minor scales have the same key tone or tonic, they belong to the same key or tonality. They differ only in *mode.* The so-called "relationship" of relative scales is entirely *visual,* while that of parallel scales is *aural.* As previously stated, all relationship of pitches is based upon the allegiance of a group of tones to a central tone. This principle determines the supremacy of the parallel over the relative relationship of major and minor scales. These relationships are shown in the following table:

| MAJOR SCALES | | MINOR SCALES | | | |
| --- | --- | --- | --- | --- | --- |
| | | *Parallel* | | *Relative* | |
| C | (0) | C | 3♭ | A | (0) |
| G | 1♯ | G | 2♭ | E | 1♯ |
| D | 2♯ | D | 1♭ | B | 2♯ |
| A | 3♯ | A | (0) | F♯ | 3♯ |
| E | 4♯ | E | 1♯ | C♯ | 4♯ |
| B | 5♯ | B | 2♯ | G♯ | 5♯ |
| F♯ | 6♯ | F♯ | 3♯ | D♯ | 6♯ |
| C♯ | 7♯ | C♯ | 4♯ | A♯ | 7♯ |
| A♭ | 4♭ | A♭ | 7♭ | F | 4♭ |
| E♭ | 3♭ | E♭ | 6♭ | C | 3♭ |
| B♭ | 2♭ | B♭ | 5♭ | G | 2♭ |
| F | 1♭ | F | 4♭ | D | 1♭ |

**33. How are Chromatic Scales written?** Chromatic scales have no signatures of their own since they are scales, not keys. They are written in relation to the prevailing key signature following the pattern for C major in example 29. Note that the tones are raised ascending, and lowered descending, except the fifth step which is written as a raised fourth step (F♯) in both directions. This formula is applied to the scale of other major keys.

*Example 38.*    Chromatic Major Scales. (a) In the key of B major. (b) In the key of D♭ major.

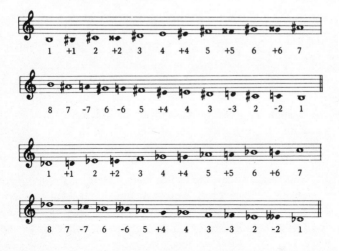

In minor keys the pattern differs slightly.

*Example 39.*   Chromatic Minor Scales. (a) In the key of E minor. (b) In
the key of D minor.

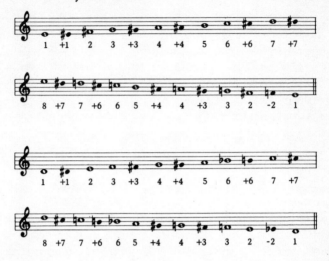

**34.   What Signatures are used for other Scales?**   In addition to the
major, minor, and chromatic scales, the medieval modes, the whole-
tone scale, and the pentatonic scales occur occasionally in Western
music. In general, all these scales use the most convenient signature, that is, the one requiring the fewest number of accidentals.

**35.   What is Tonality?**   Tonality is a broad term used to denote
tonal organization around a central tone to which all other tones are
related. It is often used somewhat loosely as equivalent to key.
Tonality may also be defined as the structural use of keys in connection with form. (See also MODULATION, Section VI, question 20,
p. 64.)

  Strictly speaking, the term *tonality* includes all tonal relationships—modal, major-minor, pentatonic, whole-tone, or chromatic.
These are all "modes," or ways of dividing the octave.

**36.   In what respects can the terms Scale (Mode), Key, and Tonality
be compared?**   These terms, though somewhat similar, are progressively broader in meaning. Scales consist only of consecutive
tones within an octave. Keys include more tonal material than scales,

and their tones have no fixed order. Tonality is the broadest term of the three and refers to the *principle* of tonal organization and its application in large movements where contrasting keys aid in outlining form.

**37. How may the Key of a Composition be identified?** The key in which a composition is written may be identified by comparing the key signature with the last note of either the melody or bass, since one of these parts usually ends on the key tone of the key in which the piece is written. Of course, the best musical way is by the ear, which soon can distinguish between the sound of major or minor melodies or chords. For example, if the key signature consists of two flats, the piece will be in either B♭ major or G minor.

*Example 40.* Songs Using Key Signatures of Two Flats. (a) The key of B♭ major. (b) The key of G minor.

**37. What is a Melody?** A melody is a logical succession of single tones related in pitch, rhythm, and design. Next to rhythm, it is the most important element in music. In fact, Mozart called it "the essence of music."

**39. What is a good Melody?** A "good" melody cannot be defined because too many intangible elements are involved. Melodies vary as widely in construction, function, and appeal as do the tastes of listeners. Their tones are related physically through natural laws and expressively through musical instinct. Aesthetic standards also change, so that today's "ugliness" may be tomorrow's "beauty," or vice versa. No absolute standards can be established. To endure, a melody must be satisfying to both the composer and the listener, whether or not its construction is understood by them. However, familiarity may lead to understanding and thus promote enjoyment.

**40. What is a Melodic Sequence?** A melodic sequence is the duplication of a tone pattern beginning on a different pitch, as in the second phrase of the song "America."

*Example 41.* A Melodic Sequence

The melody of measures 1 and 2 above is called a *figure;* the melody of measures 3 and 4 is called a *sequence* because it duplicates the figures beginning on a different (lower) pitch. This sequence is exact. A modified sequence occurs at the beginning of "America."

*Example 42.* A Modified Sequence

Sequences promote both unity and continuity in music. Because of excessive use before 1900, the device is less used today.

**41. What other Melodic devices are used?** Other melodic devices are inversion, augmentation, and diminution. Note the application of these devices to the following melody:

*Example 43.* The Basic Melody

French Folk Song

Twin - kle, twin - kle, Lit - tle star! How I won-der what you are!

A. *Inversion* reverses the direction of each interval in the melody, thus turning the melody upside down:

*Example 44.* Inversion of the Melody

B. *Augmentation* doubles the note values when played in the same tempo, thus broadening the effect of the melodic line:

*Example 45.* Augmentation of the Melody

C. *Diminution* halves the note values in the same tempo, thus shortening the melodic line:

*Example 46.* Diminution of the Melody

Other artificial devices used are *retrogression* (playing the melody backwards) and *inversion of retrogression,* but they are not immediately apparent to the listener.

# Summary—Single-Tone Relationships

Musical tones are organized in relation to time and pitch. Time relationships were discussed in Section III. Pitch relationships are organized on the principle of *tonality*, the aural supremacy of one tone in a group of related tones within an octave. This grouping of related tones has three names which have similar but progressively broader meanings: (1) the term *scale*, which refers only to the alphabetical order of tones; (2) the term *key*, referring to the relationship of all twelve tones to the principal tone; and (3) the term *tonality*, which, though often synonymous with key, refers more specifically to the key scheme of an entire composition.

With any given scale, key, or tonality, there is a choice of mode—of the tones which make up the group. Music is written usually in the *major* or *minor* mode though there are many other modes possible. The terms *major* and *minor* mean literally "greater" and "lesser." The prevalent major and minor scales are based upon the medieval Ionian and Aeolian modes respectively. The *major scale*, whose pattern corresponds to the white keys of the piano beginning on C, consists of whole steps except between its third and fourth and seventh and eighth degrees, which are half steps. Historically, the pattern of the *minor scale* corresponds to the white keys of the piano beginning on A. Aurally, however, the distinctive feature of the minor scale is the fact that its third step is one half tone lower than that of the major scale beginning on the same pitch. The upper part of the minor scale has three forms: the *harmonic*, lowered third and sixth degrees; the *melodic*, lowered third degree; and the *pure* or *natural*, lowered third, sixth, and seventh degrees. The melodic form is used when the sixth and seventh steps occur consecutively, otherwise the harmonic form is used. The natural minor is used chiefly in modal melodies. The patterns of the major and minor scales may be constructed beginning on any one of the twelve pitches in the octave.

Scale steps have letter, number, syllable, and functional names. The functional names show the relation of the other scale steps to the principal or "home" tone: (1) tonic or key tone, (2) supertonic, (3) mediant, (4) subdominant, (5) dominant, (6) submediant, and (7) leading tone.

The word *diatonic* refers to music using exclusively the tones of the major, minor, or modal scales. On the other hand, the term *chromatic* refers generally to music which contains tones foreign to the prevailing major or minor scale. It also refers to the chromatic scale which consists of all twelve pitches within the octave used consecutively. Twelve pitches are common to all keys; hence, they must be spelled according to the context. There are no chromatic keys or tonalities; entire compositions are not written solely in the chromatic scale unless they are in one of the twentieth-century "atonal" idioms.

A *key signature* is a composite symbol indicating the *accidentals* needed to maintain the scale pattern when major or minor scales begin on any tone except C and A respectively. The accidentals which form the signature affect all pitches of the same name irrespective of register. There are seven "sharp" signatures and seven "flat" signatures for major scales. The minor scales "borrow" the most convenient major signature, the one corresponding to the lowered third step of the minor scale. Major and minor scales having the same key tone or tonic are called *parallel* scales; those using the same signature are termed *relative* scales. Aurally, parallel scales are more closely related than the so-called relative scales. Scales which may be written using either sharps or flats, for example, F♯ and G♭, are called *enharmonic* scales. There are three enharmonic major and three enharmonic minor scales.

Musical
Relationships
— Combined Tones

In Section V, we considered the relationships of single tones, tones heard consecutively. In this section we will consider the relationships of combined tones, tones heard simultaneously. Specifically, we will consider intervals, harmony, and counterpoint.

**1. What is an Interval?** An interval in music is the difference in pitch between tones. These tones may be heard either consecutively or together. When heard consecutively, they form a *melodic* interval; when heard together, the interval is *harmonic*.

**2. How are Intervals classified?** Intervals are classified in two ways: in relation to their size and to their quality. The *size* of an interval corresponds to the number of staff degrees which it includes, counting the lower tone as one. Thus, C-G is a fifth because it includes five letters (C, D, E, F, G) or staff degrees. The numerical names of intervals are prime (or unison), second, third, and so forth.

The *quality* of an interval is determined by its relationship to the major scales beginning on the lower tone of the interval. Thus, an interval built on D is measured in the scale of D major; and one built on E-flat (E♭), in the E-flat major scale. The qualitative names of intervals are: perfect, major, minor, augmented, and diminished.

**3.  How are Intervals measured?**   Intervals are measured only to the octave inclusive. Beyond the octave a new series is usually begun. Occasionally ninths, tenths, or larger intervals are used, but they are treated as if they were an octave less and are known as *compound intervals*. Thus, C-D, when adjacent, form a simple second, but when separated by an octave they form a compound second, or a ninth.

**4.  How are Intervals Designated?**   Intervals are designated qualitatively, thus:

**A.** *Perfect*—when the upper tone is the first, fourth, fifth, or eighth scale degree of the lower tone

**B.** *Major*—when the upper tone is the second, third, sixth, or seventh scale degree of the major scale of the lower tone

**C.** *Minor*—one half-tone smaller than major intervals

**D.** *Diminished*—one half-tone smaller than perfect and minor intervals

**E.** *Augmented*—one half-tone larger than perfect and major intervals

The perfect and major intervals built on middle C are as follows:

*Example 47*.   The Perfect and Major Intervals Built on Middle C. The ninth and tenth intervals are rare.

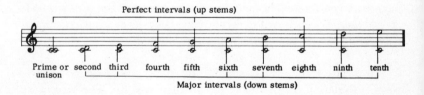

Note that the use of *accidentals* changes the quality, but not the number-name of the interval. Thus, C-G♭, C-G, and C-G♯ are all fifths, though of different quality: diminished, perfect, and augmented respectively.

Intervals may also be *doubly augmented* or *doubly diminished* by being altered an additional half tone in the direction indicated by their respective titles.

*Example 48.*   Doubly Altered Intervals. (a) A doubly augmented fifth. (b) A doubly diminished fourth.

The origin of the qualitative names for intervals is fairly clear except possibly the term *perfect,* which is so named because of the close acoustical relationship of its tones. Perfect intervals are also "double majors" in the sense that each tone is to be found in the major scale of the other tone. The term *minor,* as applied to intervals, simply means *lesser* and does not refer to minor scales.

**5.   How are Intervals Inverted?**   Intervals are inverted by reversing the order of their tones, for example, the fifth C-G when inverted becomes the fourth G-C. The concept of inversion aids in naming difficult intervals. To determine the effect of inversion on any interval, subtract the number of the interval from nine, for example, a fifth inverted becomes a fourth. When inverted, the quality of an interval is reversed except for perfect intervals which remain perfect. The following table illustrates the inversion of intervals:

| octave ⎫ | | ⎧ prime |
|---|---|---|
| seventh | | second |
| sixth | | third |
| fifth | inverted | fourth |
| fourth ⎬ | becomes | ⎨ fifth |
| third | | sixth |
| second | | seventh |
| prime ⎭ | | ⎩ octave |

**6.   What are Consonant and Dissonant Intervals?**   All intervals are classified as being consonant or dissonant according to the ratio of their vibrations, thus:

**A.** consonant intervals—all perfect intervals and major and minor thirds and sixths

**B.** dissonant intervals—all others

This division is entirely arbitrary and is made solely for purposes of classification. A detailed knowledge of intervals is not essential for the amateur.

**7.   What is the Function of Dissonance?**   The function of dissonance in music is to serve as a foil for consonance, that is, to provide variety in the texture. Consonance and dissonance are very important musical concepts. They are best defined in aesthetic rather than in acoustical terms. Dissonance refers to a sense of activity or tension and consonance to a feeling of repose or relaxation. A dissonance is *resolved* or completed when it is followed by a consonance. Note first that consonance and dissonance are relative, arbitrary terms which are sometimes difficult to distinguish aurally; second, that they should never be defined in terms of ugliness or beauty since what is ugly to one listener may be beautiful to another.

**8.   What is Harmony?**   Harmony is a vertical aspect of music. It consists of a series of related structures called *chords*. Harmony, which began to develop intensively only after 1600, was the last element to appear in Western music.

**9.   What is a Chord and how is it built?**   Traditionally, a chord is a group of three to seven different tones built upward in a series of thirds, or reducible to thirds; hence, it is actually a combination of two or more intervals. For example, if the first six tones of the *Star-Spangled Banner* are played together, they form the chord Bb-D-F. The lowest tone (Bb) is the *root* of the chord, D is its *third,* and F is its *fifth.*

*Example 49.*   A Melody which Builds a Chord

**10.   How are Chords named?**   Chords are named or classified according to their roots, size, and quality, as illustrated by the chord in example 49:

**A.** From its root:
$\left\{\begin{array}{l}\text{letter name: B}\flat \\ \text{number name: I} \\ \text{functional name: tonic}\end{array}\right\}$
(See example 51)

**B.** From its size: three-tone chord, a triad (See example 50)

**C.** From its intervals: quality names
$\left\{\begin{array}{l}\text{major (See question 16)} \\ \text{consonant (See question 17)}\end{array}\right.$

Thus, each chord actually has six names to describe its various attributes and characteristics.

**11. How many different Tones may a Chord have?** A chord may contain from three to seven different tones, the latter consisting of every tone in the scale arranged in thirds. A three-tone chord is called a *triad*, regardless of the number of repeated tones that it may contain. Chords may be extended by adding more tones in thirds until the first tone, or the *root*, is reached again, thus:

*Example 50.* Chord Sizes

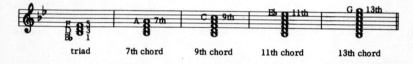

Note that the additional tones are numbered 7, 9, 11, 13, according to their distance from the chord root.

**12. Upon what Tones are Chords built?** Chords are built using any scale tone as the root. They are named from either the letter, number, or scale name of their root. Thus, the triads in B-flat major are named:

*Example 51.* Triads in the Key of B-flat Major

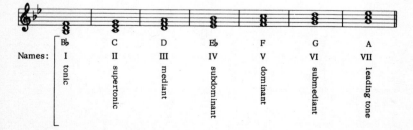

**13.  What types of Chords are the most used?**  Triads, seventh chords, and ninth chords are the most frequently used types of chord and occur in that order of frequency. Chords of the eleventh and thirteenth are very rare. The chord of the fifteenth is simply a chord of the thirteenth with its root repeated, or "doubled," and does not form a new chord.

**14.  In what order may Chord Tones be arranged?**  Chord tones may be arranged in any order. The chord is said to be *inverted* when any other tone than the root is the lowest tone. These are the two inversions of the B-flat major triad:

*Example 52.*    Two Inversions of the B-flat Major Triad

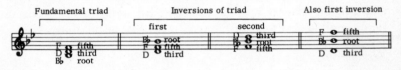

A chord has as many inversions as the number of thirds it contains.

**15.  How are Chords related?**  Chords are related through the scale degrees used as their roots. Since these roots are related, the chords erected on them are related also. The simplest relationship is between chords whose roots are a perfect fifth apart. (See question 21, Section V, p. 42.) The most natural progression or sequence of chords is when their roots move downward a perfect fifth toward the tonic (I) chord, except the subdominant (IV) chord whose root must move upward a fifth to reach the tonic chord. Note, however, that the IV chord very often progresses up one step to the V chord.

*Example 53.*    The Progression of Chord Roots in C Major

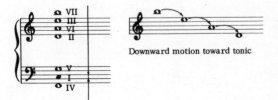

Downward motion toward tonic

**16.  What determines the quality of Chords?**  The quality of chords is determined by the intervals which they contain, counting upward from the root of the chord. On this basis, triads may be major, minor, augmented, or diminished. Major and minor triads are named from the quality of their first third. A diminished triad is named from the quality of its fifth. An augmented triad is named from the quality of its fifth.

| | | |
|---|---|---|
| A major triad | a major third and a perfect fifth | |
| A minor triad | a minor third and a perfect fifth | from its root. |
| A diminished triad | contains { a minor third and a diminished fifth | |
| An augmented triad | a major third and an augmented fifth | |

*Example 54.*    The Qualities of Triads in the Key of C Major

*Example 55.*    The Qualities of Triads in the Harmonic Form of the C Minor Scale

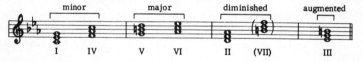

The qualities of seventh and larger chords are so varied that it is not necessary to list them here. However, the two most commonly used seventh chords are:

*Example 56.*    The Two Common Seventh Chords in the Key of C Minor

The dominant-seventh (V⁷) occurs in both modes; the diminished-seventh (VII⁷) occurs only in the minor as a diatonic chord.

**17. How are Chords classified in relation to Consonance and Dissonance?** *A chord is dissonant if it contains a dissonant interval.* Hence, major and minor triads are the only consonant chords. Augmented and diminished triads and all chords larger than a triad are dissonant.

**18. May Chords be chromatically altered?** Yes, all types of chords are subject to the chromatic alteration of one or more of their tones. In general, chromatic chords are used to *embellish* or decorate diatonic chords, just as chromatic tones are used in melodies for embellishment. The types of chromatic chords are so numerous and complex that a standard harmony text should be consulted for their explanation.

**19. How is Chromaticism related to Tonality?** The relationship of chromaticism to tonality is an interesting one since it involves a broad concept of tonality. The basic principle of Western music, the allegiance of a group of tones to a central tone, is called *tonality*. To *chromaticize* means to "color" the music with tones foreign to the group of related tones or the key.

**20. What is Modulation?** Modulation is the process by which a new key center or tonality is reached and established. Chromaticism may *suggest* a new key, but a genuine change of key (modulation) is usually not made unless the new implied key is confirmed by several strong, conclusive chords known as a *cadence*. The concluding chords of any composition are an example of such a cadence. Modulation seldom occurs without a strong cadence in the new key. Two melodies illustrate the point: the first phrase of the "Star-Spangled Banner" and the beginning of the Christmas hymn "Adeste Fidelis." The first illustration does not modulate to F major in spite of the E-natural (♮) in the melody because of the lack of harmonic support.

*Example 57.* Modulation. (a) The *suggestion* of a new key. The asterisks indicate chromatic, not modulatory chords. (b) Modulation which establishes a new key.

a)

Francis Scott Key, *The Star Spangled Banner*

Oh__ say can you see by the dawn's ear - ly light

*Adeste Fideles*

In example 57b .there are no accidentals in the melody, but the strong series of chords serve to establish the key of E major in measure 8. The modulatory cadence is on the word "Bethlehem." The chords in measures 7 and 8 form the necessary cadence which sets up the new key of E major.

It is here that a wider concept of tonality emerges, that of *the relationship of keys to each other.* Keys as well as chords are related by fifths. (See example 53.) By the use of certain chord progressions or patterns, a new key or tonality may be established. Thus, the wider definition of tonality is the particular organization of keys around the home key of a composition similar to the relationship of chords to their home or tonic chord. This use of tonality is one of the most important factors in musical form.

The subject of modulation and the relationship of tonalities is an interesting and complex one. The reader is advised to consult a standard work on harmony for a more complete explanation of them.

**21. Do all Simultaneous Tones form Chords?**   In simple music a group of tones sounded together generally forms a chord. However, this group of tones may consist either of chord tones only, or of both chord and nonchord tones. Tones which do not belong to the chord are called *nonharmonic* tones. Usually they are adjacent to chord tones and are identified and named by the way in which they move to or from the nearest chord tone. The principal types of nonharmonic tones are: the neighboring tone, the suspension, the anticipation, and the appoggiatura. (For definitions of these and other types, see the Glossary.)

Recognition of nonharmonic tones is only possible in reference to the harmonic background of a composition. The nonharmonic tones are most easily heard in the melody, though they may occur in lower parts as well. In the following example, the first measure contains four nonharmonic tones enclosed in circles, while the second measure consists entirely of chord tones:

*Example 58.*   Nonharmonic and Chord Tones

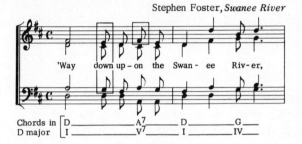

At the word *down* the tonal combination D, G, C♯, E does not form a chord. This is because the three upper voices (G, C♯, E) do not belong to the D chord which is implied by the bass tone and reinforced by the preceding and following D, F♯, A chords. At the last syllable of *upon,* the tonal combination does suggest the chord A, C♯, E, G which is confirmed by the next chord. In this case, the melody tone F♯ is the only nonharmonic tone. Recognition of nonharmonic tones requires considerable experience in musical analysis.

Nonharmonic tones enrich the texture of the music and aid in giving it a sense of forward motion. The urgency of nonharmonic tones is due to the fact that they are always dissonant and demand resolution, which suggests motion.

**22.   What is Counterpoint?**   Counterpoint is the art of combining two or more melodies. The term comes from the Latin phrase *punctus contra punctum*—that is, point against point, meaning note against note. Historically, counterpoint preceded harmony, but since about 1600, both textures have been used, either together or separately. Counterpoint is a serious art used skillfully by composers to give a rich and varied texture to their music. Probably the most familiar example of counterpoint is a *round,* for example, "Three Blind Mice." There are many simple folksongs that can be treated similarly.

*Example 59.* A Folk Song Treated as a Round

Folk Song

Twin - kle, twin - kle, lit - tle star, How I

Twin - kle, twin - kle lit - tle

won - der what you are. Up a - bove the

star, How I won - der what you are.

The principle of the *round* or *canon* is also used in instrumental music.

*Example 60.* The Principle of the Round or Canon in Instrumental Music

Bach, *Two-part Invention in F Major*

Franck, *Sonata for Violin and Piano*
Fourth movement

*Allegretto poco mosso*

Beethoven, *Symphony No.4*, First Movement

Perhaps a more familiar example of counterpoint is a "counter-melody" which is often played by the trombone or piccolo in band marches or by a violin as an obbligato to a song. When such a melody is added to choral music, it is called a *descant*.

**23. How do Harmony and Counterpoint differ?** Harmony and counterpoint differ chiefly in the way in which tones are combined and heard. They are organized on different principles. In harmony the tones are planned vertically, while in counterpoint the organization is horizontal. Of course, vertical combinations of tones are produced in counterpoint, but the organizing factor is chiefly on the melodic line of each part (or voice). In harmony we have a melody supported by chords; in counterpoint, a series of simultaneous melodies which only incidentally form chords. The technical names for these two types of texture are *homophonic* for chordal music and *polyphonic* for contrapuntal music. A hymn or a piece like Dvořak's "Humoreske" is homophonic in texture, while a round, a canon, or a fugue is polyphonic in texture. However, these two textures are often intermingled as in Schumann's "Träumerei" ("Dreaming") from his *Scenes of Childhood, op.* 15.

# Summary—Combined-Tone Relationships

Two tones heard either consecutively or together form an *interval*. Melodies consist of *melodic* intervals and chords of *harmonic* intervals. The two names of an interval are based upon the distance between its tones. It has a number name, counting the lower tone as 1, and a quality name, indicating the relationship of the upper tone to the major scale of the lower tone.

Primes, fourths, fifths, and octaves which occur in the major scale of the lower tone are called *perfect* intervals. Seconds, thirds, sixths, and sevenths are called *major, minor, diminished,* or *augmented* intervals according to their deviation from the major scale of the lower tone.

Perfect intervals and major and minor thirds and sixths are called *consonant* intervals; all others are termed *dissonant.* In general, consonance and dissonance are relative terms meaning simply *relaxation* and *tension.* A dissonance is *resolved* (or completed) when it is followed by a consonance. For our purpose, intervals are useful chiefly for determining the quality of chords.

A *chord* is a combination of three or more different letters representing pitches than can be arranged in thirds. Counting upwards in thirds from the bottom, the tones of a chord are called the root, third, fifth, seventh, and others. A chord has a generic name derived from its size. Thus, three-tone chords are called *triads.* All other chords are named from their largest interval, counting upwards in thirds from the root.

A chord also has four specific names, three derived from its root and one from its intervallic structure. The root names are: a staff letter, a scale number, and a scale name, for example, C, I, and *tonic* in the key of C. The qualitative name is based upon the intervallic structure of the chord, for example, major triad, diminished-seventh chord. The consonance or dissonance of a chord depends upon the intervals which it contains. Major and minor triads are consonant chords; all other chords are dissonant because they contain one or more dissonant intervals.

Chords are related through their roots, the simplest relationship being between two chords whose roots are a perfect fifth apart. The relative importance of a chord depends upon the distance of its root from the tonic, or key tone, measured in perfect fifths. Hence, the most important triads are the I (tonic), the V (dominant), and the IV (subdominant), respectively. These are primary chords while all other chords are classed as secondary. The most important seventh chord is the V⁷ (dominant-seventh chord) which is the only diatonic chord belonging exclusively to one tonality.

Chromatic chords are, in general, embellishments of diatonic chords. Their structure is similar to that of diatonic chords, but their progression is dependent upon the chord embellished. The general effect of chromatic chords is to expand the tonality within which they occur. They are intimately related to *modulation*, a change of tonality or key center. A study of chromatic chords properly belongs in advanced harmony.

Simultaneous tones usually form chords, but not always. Tones that occur with a chord, but which do not belong to it, are called *nonharmonic tones*. They can be identified by arranging a group of simultaneous tones in a series of thirds. Those tones which do not fit into this pattern are nonharmonic (nonchord) tones. Essentially all nonharmonic tones are adjacent to chord tones and are named according to how they progress.

The tones of a chord may appear in any order. When any tone other than the root is the lowest tone, the chord is said to be *inverted*. Triads have two inversions, and seventh chords have three.

*Counterpoint* is the art of combining two or more melodies. Basically, the organization of counterpoint is horizontal while that of harmony is vertical. The texture of contrapuntal music is called *polyphonic* and that of harmonic music is termed *homophonic*. Since 1600, the texture of Western music has become chiefly homophonic, though both textures are often found now in the same composition.

# SECTION SEVEN | Musical Relationships — Forms

We have considered the musical relationships of combined tones in the previous section. In this section, we will consider the broader aspects of the relationships of combined tones—musical ideas and their relationships in musical compositions—that is *form*.

**1. What is Form in Music?**  Form is the organization of the total time required to perform a composition by an ordered arrangement of the composer's musical ideas. It is similar to the plot of a story. The composer's problem is how to achieve a balance between unity and variety. He does so by using enough repetition to give unity but sufficient new material for variety. Only the formal principles of homophonic music are discussed here since polyphonic music is organized on different principles.

**2. What is a Phrase?**  The basic unit of form is the *phrase*, a musical idea ended by a point of rest called a *cadence*. Homophonic compositions consist of a series of phrases just as a book is made up of sentences. In fact, musical phrases and phrases in language are quite similar in function. Phrases vary in length, although many consist of four measures. The melody set to the line of poetry, "Drink to me only with thine eyes and I will pledge with mine," is a four-measure phrase.

**3. What is a Period?** Two phrases in the relationship of question-and-answer form a *period*. The beginning of "Annie Laurie" is a good example of a period.

*Example 61.* Two Phrases Forming a Period

The principle of the period is sometimes expanded into a *double period*. In this form, phrases one and three and two and four are usually similar, as in "Flow Gently, Sweet Afton."

**4. What are the principal designs in Homophonic Music?** The principal designs are the *binary* and *ternary* forms. Compositions usually contain more than one basic musical idea. For example, "My Country 'tis of Thee" has two. The first begins with the words of the title and the second with the line "Land where my fathers died." This pattern is known as the *binary* or *two-part song form*, its parts being represented by the letters *A-B*. Brahms' "Cradle Song" and "My Bonnie Lies over the Ocean" are familiar examples of binary forms.

When a composition has only two basic ideas but ends with a repetition of the first it is known as a *ternary* or *three-part song form*, represented by the letters *A-B-A*. Many familiar songs such as "Annie Laurie" or "Drink to Me Only with Thine Eyes" are examples of the ternary form.

The *A-B-A* form is probably the most basic design in music. It is used in marches, minuets, mazurkas, and other dance forms which consist of two contrasting dances, ending with a repetition of the first dance. In such a design the second dance is called the *trio*. The same *A-B-A* form greatly expanded is used for the large compound forms such as the *sonata-allegro* design (often the first movement of a sonata or a symphony) and for the *scherzo,* which developed historically from the *minuet.*

Obviously more alternating ideas can be introduced, in which case, the pattern expands, for example, *A-B-A-C-A.* This is the design of compositions called *rondos*—which simply means that the principal idea returns periodically.

The form of vocal music is somewhat freer than that of instrumental music because the words give additional continuity or design to the music. However, much vocal music is in the *A-B* or *A-B-A* form, as are the songs cited above. The form of choral music tends to be more free than that of either instrumental or solo vocal music. Music that is predominantly polyphonic in texture usually consists of a number of closely related "sections" which do not make a typical form. There are compositional *devices,* such as the *variation* and the *fugue,* which are sometimes classified as "forms."

The principle of musical form is simple—a balance between unity and variety; but its application is sometimes complex. For details the student should consult a standard work on the subject.

# Summary—Form Relationships

*Form in music* is the organization and sequence of musical ideas. It is tonal design. Form results from a balance between unity (similarity) and variety (difference). Unity is achieved through repetition; variety, through contrast. The basic unit of form in music is the *phrase*, a musical idea ended by a point of rest called a *cadence*. Two phrases in the relation of question-and-answer are called a *period*.

Compositions may contain only one basic idea, but usually include two or more. Two contrasting ideas result in the *binary* or *two-part song form* represented by the letters A-B. A return to the first idea (A) results in the *ternary* or *three-part song form* represented by the letters A-B-A. Large compound forms—the *sonata-allegro, minuet, scherzo,* or *march* forms—also are based upon the ternary or *A-B-A* principle, which is the most common design in music or any of the other arts. Further digressions and returns (A-B-A-C-A, and so on) follow the pattern of the *rondo* form. The form of vocal music is largely determined by the words, although many of the forms cited above are to be found in solo and ensemble vocal music. Polyphonic music is usually sectional in form. Certain compositional procedures, such as the variation and the fugue, are sometimes termed "forms." Form gives music continuity and meaning, and hence some design or form is essential for all types of music.

Musical
References

## A Glossary of Commonly Used Musical Terms

**a cappella**  Unaccompanied choral singing.

**accelerando**  Gradually increasing the speed.

**acciaccatura**  A short grace note.

**accidental**  A notational symbol (♯,♭,x,♭♭,♮) to indicate an alteration of the prevailing pitch. See p. 17.

**adagio**  A slow, leisurely tempo; faster than *lento*, slower than *andante*.

**ad libitum**  At will; at the liberty of the performer.

**agitato**  Agitated.

**al fine**  To the end.

**alla breve**  (¢). An indication of duple meter, $\frac{2}{2}$ ,usually at a quick tempo.

**allargando**  Slowing down, broadening and increasingly louder.

**allegretto**  A lively tempo; quicker than *andante,* not so fast as *allegro.*

**allegro**  A quick, rapid, or brisk tempo; literally: merry.

**alto**  The lower of the two divisions of women's or boys' voices.

**amoroso**  Lovingly.

**andante**  A very moderate tempo; literally: walking or going.

**andantino**   Usually a little quicker than *andante*.

**animato**   Animated.

**anticipation**   A nonharmonic tone which anticipates a harmonic tone of the following harmony.

**appassionato**   Passionate, intense.

**appoggiatura**   A nonharmonic tone on the beat, approached by leap and resolved by step.

**aria**   A vocal solo in opera, oratorio, or cantata.

**arpeggio**   Harplike; notes of a chord played in swift succession rather than simultaneously.

**a tempo**   Return to the original tempo.

**atonality**   The absence of tonality.

**bar**   A vertical line drawn on the staff to mark off measures; the term is incorrectly used to denote the measures themselves. See p. 11.

**baritone**   The male voice between the bass and tenor; also, a band instrument of the brass family.

**bass**   The lowest male adult voice. Also, the lowest instrumental part of a composition.

**beat**   Pulse; the temporal unit of a musical composition; one of the equal metric divisions of a measure. See p. 10.

**bel canto**   A lyric, vocal style; the opposite of dramatic; literally: beautiful song.

**bravura**   A virtuoso style or brilliant passage requiring skillful technique; literally: courage.

**brillante**   Brilliantly, gay, showy.

**broken chords, broken octaves**   Chords or octaves whose notes are played in succession, not simultaneously.

**cadence**   A sequence of tones or chords closing a phrase or a composition. A point of rest. See p. 64, 71.

**cadenza**   An ornamental and brilliant solo passage introduced toward the end of a composition which allows the performer to display his virtuosity.

**canon**   A melody sung in turn by two or more voices, each voice overlapping the one before; a round is a type of canon.

**cantabile**   In a singing style.

**cantata**   A vocal work of smaller scale than an oratorio which is either sacred or secular in nature.

**cantilena** Of lyric rather than dramatic character; graceful.

**capriccioso** Capriciously, fancifully.

**chord** A combination of three or more tones according to harmonic principles. See p. 60.

**coda, codetta** A short concluding passage.

**coloratura** A florid passage. Also, the highest female voice, capable of executing florid passages.

**con anima** With animation.

**con brio** With briskness.

**concertmaster** The chief, or leading, violinist of an orchestra who often assists the conductor.

**concerto** A piece of several contrasting movements for one or more solo instruments with orchestra.

**con moto** With motion.

**contralto** The lower alto voice.

**counterpoint** The art of combining melodies. See p. 66.

**crescendo** Gradually increasing in volume.

**da capo (D. C.)** From the beginning. This term indicates that the composition is to be repeated from the beginning to the place marked *fine* (end).

**dal segno (D. S.)** From the sign. This term indicates that a part of the composition is to be repeated beginning with the sign 𝄋 .

**decrescendo** Gradually decreasing in volume.

**descant** (or discant) An ornamental vocal melody added to a vocal composition. See **obbligato.**

**diminuendo** Gradually decreasing in volume.

**dolce** Sweetly.

**dynamic markings** Markings to indicate changes in volume.

**enharmonic** Different spellings for identical pitches, for example, E♭ and D♯ . See p. 19.

**entr' acte** Music played between the acts of a play or opera.

**eroica** Heroic.

**espressivo** Expressively.

**falsetto** A false or artificial voice; very high head tones in the adult male voice.

**fermata** A symbol (⌢) indicating that the note or rest is to be held or prolonged; a pause.

**finale**  The last movement of a compound composition. Also the closing number of an operatic act.

**fine**  The end.

**fioritura**  Melodic embellishments.

**forte** (*f*)  Loud, strong.

**fortissimo** (*ff*)  Very loud.

**forzando, forzato** (*fz*)  Forcing, forced, meaning that a note or chord is to be strongly accented.

**fugue**  A contrapuntal composition based on a theme (subject) whose second entry (answer), in a different voice, is a perfect fifth higher or a perfect fourth lower.

**fuoco**  Fire, spirit.


**giocoso**  Playful.

**glissando**  Gliding, sliding; an effect produced by sliding the finger quickly along the strings, keys, or positions (of a trombone).

**grace note**  A short note printed in a small size, whose time value is not included in the measure but is to be subtracted from the preceding or following note. Its performance varies according to type.

**grandioso**  Grand, majestic, pompous.

**grave**  The slowest musical tempo; solemn.

**grazioso**  Gracefully.


**harmonics**  Faint tones produced by the vibration of segments of the vibrating medium. See p. 7.

**harmony**  The study of chords and chord progressions.

**homophony**  A type of musical texture in which a melody is supported by chords; sameness of sound. See p. 68.


**inharmonic tone**  See **nonharmonic tone.**

**intensity**  Volume; "loudness" or "softness." See p. 6.

**interlude**  An inserted musical passage.

**intermezzo**  A broad term meaning today either an intermediate or independent orchestral composition, or a short piano piece.

**interval**  The difference in pitch between two tones. See p. 57.

**inversion**  A change of an octave in the pitch of one or more notes in an interval or chord.


**key**  The lever that is moved to make the instrument produce sound. Also, the tonal center of a composition. See p. 42.

**largamente**    Broadly.

**larghetto**    A tempo not quite so slow as *largo*.

**larghissimo**    Slower than *largo*.

**largo**    A slow, broad tempo, almost as slow as *grave*, slower than *lento*.

**legato**    Smooth and connected; very often indicated by a slur over or under the notes.

**lento**    A slow tempo between *adagio* and *largo*.


**madrigal**    A secular choral composition in contrapuntal style for five or six voices (fifteenth to eighteenth centuries).

**meno**    Less.

**metronome**    A mechanical or electrical device producing ticking sounds which can be adjusted to various rates of speeds.

**mezzo forte** (*mf*)    Half as loud as forte.

**mezzo piano** (*mp*)    Half as loud as piano.

**mezzo-soprano**    The female voice between the alto and the soprano.

**mode**    The manner of organizing tones within the octave. Also a type of scale. See p. 36.

**moderato**    A moderate tempo, between *andantino* and *allegretto*.

**modulation**    The change of tonal center within a composition. See p. 64.

**molto**    Much.

**monophony**    A single melodic line without accompaniment.

**morendo**    Dying away.

**motet**    A sacred choral composition in contrapuntal style contemporaneous with the madrigal.

**motive**    The smallest unit of a musical idea.

**mute**    A device used to soften or muffle the tone of an instrument.


**neighboring tone**    A nonharmonic tone, either upper or lower, which returns to the same harmonic tone. An auxiliary tone.

**nonharmonic tone**    A tone foreign to (and dissonant with) the momentary harmony with which it is sounding; for example, the suspension, passing tone, neighboring tone, anticipation, or appoggiatura.


**obbligato**    An added ornamental instrumental part, in contrast to a descant. See **descant**.

**octave**   The interval between any tone and the tone next above or below that has the same letter name; the distance between the first and eighth degrees of a major or minor scale. See p. 16.

**octave-marks** (8ᵛᵃ and 8ᵛᵃ *bassa*)   Symbols indicating that the note or notes are to be played an octave higher or an octave lower respectively.

**opera**   A work that is usually sung throughout, with orchestral accompaniment, scenery, and acting.

**opus (op.)**   An opus number indicates the chronological position of a composition within a composer's total output.

**oratorio**   An extended dramatic composition usually based upon a Scriptural text. It consists of choruses and solos accompanied by orchestra, but without the use of scenery or costumes.

**partials**   See **harmonics**. See also p. 7.

**passing tone**   A nonharmonic tone passing by step between two harmonic tones.

**pedal point**   A sustained note, usually in the bass, over which changing harmonies are heard.

**pianissimo** (*pp*)   Very softly.

**piano** (*p*)   Softly.

**pitch**   The "highness" or "lowness" of a musical tone. See p. 6.

**più**   More.

**pizzicato**   Plucked, rather than bowed.

**poco a poco**   Little by little.

**polyphony**   A musical texture composed of independent melodic lines which support one another.

**polytonality**   The simultaneous sounding of two or more tonalities.

**prestissimo**   The fastest tempo in music; as fast as possible.

**presto**   A very quick tempo; faster than *allegro*, but slower than *prestissimo*.

**primo**   Principal; first.

**quality**   See **timbre**.

**rallentando (rall.)**   Gradually becoming slower.

**ritardando (rit.)**   Gradually slower and slower.

**ritenuto**   Retained, kept back; an immediate reduction of speed.

**rubato**   An elasticity or flexibility of the steady beat for expressive purposes; literally: robbed.

**scale** A series of the tones comprised within an octave arranged in consecutive order of pitch. See p. 35.

**scherzando** Playfully, jestingly.

**scherzo** Usually a lively instrumental composition in triple meter belonging to a sonata, symphony, quartet, or other musical forms.

**semitone** The smallest interval used in Western music; a half step. See p. 16.

**senza** Without.

**sforzando** (*sfz* or *sfp*) Forcing; sudden emphasis on a single note or chord. The same as **forzando.**

**signature** *Key signature*—the composite of accidentals (sharps or flats) placed on the staff to indicate the key of the composition. See p. 44. *Time signature*—two numbers placed at the beginning of a composition to indicate the number of beats per measure (top number) and the note value equivalent to one beat (bottom number). See p. 25.

**slur** The sign ⌒ placed over or under two or more notes of different pitches to indicate that the passage is to be played *legato*.

**smorzando** Dying away.

**sonata** A composition for a solo instrument, or for a solo instrument with piano accompaniment in several contrasting movements. Often the term is used to refer to the sonata-allegro form, which consists of three principal sections: exposition, development, and recapitulation.

**soprano** The higher of the two divisions of women's or boys' voices, or the highest member of a family of instruments.

**sordino** Mute.

**sostenuto** Sustained.

**sotto voce** Under the voice; almost whispering.

**staccato** Detached, separate. Notes made as short as possible; the opposite of legato. Indicated by dots above or below the notes.

**stringendo** Increasing in speed and intensity.

**subito** Suddenly, immediately.

**suspension** A nonharmonic tone, resolved by step, held over from the preceding chord.

**symphony** A composition for orchestra, usually consisting of several contrasting movements. Similar in structure to the sonata.

**syncopation** Accenting an ordinarily unaccented part of a measure, thus changing the normal accent. See p. 10.

**tempo**    The pace at which a composition is to be performed. See p. 12, 27.

**tenor**    The highest male adult voice.

**tenuto**    Held; sustained for its full value.

**tetrachord**    Four consecutive pitches, for example, C, D, E, F. Major and minor scales consist of two tetrachords.

**theme**    A musical idea that serves as the basis for a composition or a section of a composition.

**tie**    A curved line joining two notes of the same pitch indicating that the second is not to be sounded again, but sustained for the value of the second note.

**timbre**    Quality, or tone color; the difference between tones of the same pitch and intensity if produced by different instruments. See p. 6.

**tonality**    Tonal organization around a central tone to which all other tones are related; loosely equivalent to *key*. See p. 50.

**tone**    A musical sound; a term applied to pitch. Also applied to the difference in pitch between two tones or the distance between notes on the staff.

**tranquillo**    Quietly.

**transcription**    The arrangement of a composition for a medium other than that for which it was originally composed.

**transposition**    The transference of an entire melody or composition from one key to another.

**tre corde**    A term used in piano music to indicate the use of the damper pedal (the pedal to the right). Literally: three strings.

**triad**    A chord of three tones, consisting of a root, third, and fifth. See p. 61.

**trill** (*tr.* ⁓⁓⁓⁓⁓⁓)    A musical embellishment, either vocal or instrumental, consisting of a given note rapidly alternating with its major or minor second above.

**triplet**    A group of three notes performed in the time of two. See p. 24.

**troppo**    Too much.

**tutti**    All; the entire number of singers or players.

**una corda (U. C.)**    A term used in piano music to indicate the use of the soft pedal (the pedal to the left). Literally: one string.

**unison**    The same pitch sounded by two or more instruments or voices.

**vibrato**   A slight fluctuation of pitch for expressive effect.
**vivace**   A quick, lively tempo.
**vivo**   Lively, spirited.
**voce**   Voice.

# A Chart of the

| Historical Eras | Representative Vocal Forms | Representative Instrumental Forms |
|---|---|---|
| *Early Christian* 350-1000 A.D. | Plain chant | |
| *Medieval and Renaissance* 850-1600 | Organum<br>Mass<br>Motet<br>Madrigal<br>Solo song | Toccata<br>Canzona<br>Ricercar<br>Dances<br>Fantasy piece |
| *Baroque* 1600-1750 | Madrigal<br>Mass<br>Motet<br>Anthem<br>Opera<br>Oratorio<br>Cantata | Sonata in several forms<br>Fugue<br>Concerto grosso<br>Solo concerto<br>Suite<br>Ballet<br>Overture<br>Chorale-prelude<br>Variations |
| *Classic* 1750-1830 | Solo song<br>Part-song<br>Mass<br>Opera<br>Oratorio | Solo concerto<br>Sonata<br>Chamber music<br>Solo piece<br>Symphony<br>Variations<br>Overture |
| *Romantic* 1830-1910 | Mass<br>Oratorio<br>Cantata<br>Opera<br>Art song<br>Part-song | Character piece<br>Sonata<br>Solo concerto<br>Symphony<br>Symphonic poem<br>Overture<br>Program music<br>Chamber music |
| *Modern* 1890- | Opera<br>Oratorio<br>Mass<br>Art song<br>Part-song | Fugue<br>Concerto grosso<br>Symphony<br>Chamber music<br>Sonata<br>Solo concerto<br>Solo piece |

# History of Music

| 100 Representative Composers (in chronological order) | | | | Historical Eras |
|---|---|---|---|---|
| | | | | *Early Christian* 350-1000 A.D. |
| Leonin Perotin Machaut Landini Dunstable Dufay | Ockeghem Obrecht Isaac Josquin Jannequin Willaert | Morales A. Gabrieli Palestrina Lassus Byrd Victoria | G. Gabrieli Morley Dowland Marenzio Gesualdo Gibbons | *Medieval and Renaissance* 850-1600 |
| Caccini Peri Sweelinck Monteverdi Frescobaldi Schuetz Carissimi Lully Buxtehude Corelli | | Pachelbel Purcell A. Scarlatti Couperin Vivaldi Telemann D. Scarlatti J. S. Bach Handel | | *Baroque* 1600-1750 |
| Pergolesi Gluck C. P. E. Bach J. Stamitz Haydn Mozart | | Cherubini Beethoven Rossini Donizetti Bellini | | *Classic* 1750-1830 |
| von Weber Schubert Berlioz Mendelssohn Chopin R. Schumann Liszt Wagner | Verdi Franck Bruckner Brahms Bizet Moussorgsky Tchaikovsky Dvořak | Grieg Rimsky-Korsakoff Puccini Wolf Mahler R. Strauss Sibelius | | *Romantic* 1830-1910 |
| Debussy Vaughan Williams Schoenberg Ives Ravel Bartok Villa-Lobos Stravinsky | Berg Riegger Varese Prokofieff Milhaud Moore Hindemith Hanson | Cowell Copland Shostakovich Barber W. Schuman Britten Stockhausen | | *Modern* 1890- |

# A Classification of Instruments

| Kind and Character of Instrument | | | General Range[1] | | | | |
|---|---|---|---|---|---|---|---|
| | | | Very high | High | Medium | Low | Very low |
| String | Bowed | | | Violin | Viola | Violoncello | Contrabass (double bass) |
| | Plucked | | Harp, Mandolin, Guitar | | | | |
| Wind | Wood-wind | Sharp-edged hole | Piccolo | Flute | | | |
| | | Reed — Single | E♭ clarinet | B♭ or A clarinet[2] / B♭ saxophone | E♭ alto saxophone[2] / B♭ or A clarinet[2] | Tenor saxophone | Bass clarinet / Baritone saxophone |
| | | Reed — Double | | Oboe[2] | English horn / Oboe[2] / Bassoon[3] | Bassoon[3] | Contrabassoon (double bassoon) / Sarrusophone |
| | Brass | Cup-shaped mouthpiece | | Trumpet / Cornet | French horn | Tenor trombone / Baritone / Euphonium | Bass trombone / Tuba / Sousaphone |
| Percussion | Definite pitch | | Timpani, Bells, Chimes, Xylophone, Marimba | | | | |
| | Indefinite pitch | | Snare drum, Bass drum, Cymbals, Tambourine, Triangle, Gongs, Castanets | | | | |
| Keyboard | Struck strings | | Piano | | | | |
| | Plucked strings | | Harpsichord | | | | |
| | Struck bars | | Celesta | | | | |
| | Wind, over sharp-edged holes or reeds, through pipes | | Organ | | | | |
| | Electronic | | | | | | |

[1] The general orchestral ranges are somewhat similar to the vocal ranges high soprano, soprano, alto, tenor, and bass; but there is much overlapping between them.

[2] These instruments are used in both the high and medium ranges.

[3] These instruments are used in both the medium and low ranges.

# Frequency Ranges
## of Instruments
## and Voices

See p. 88

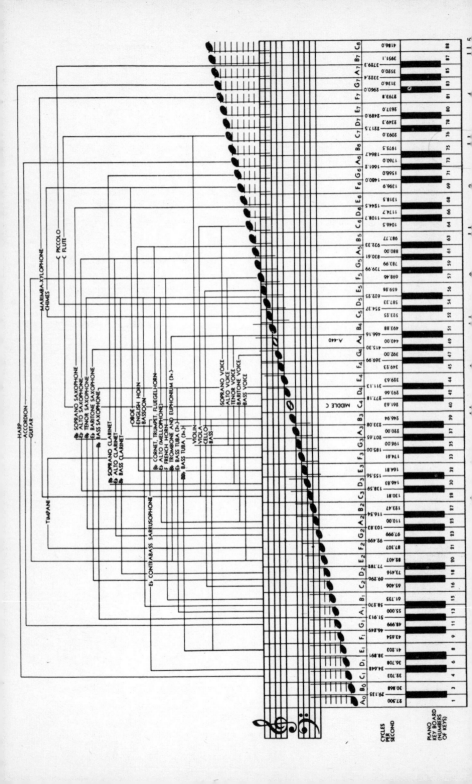

# A Selected Bibliography

## STANDARD REFERENCE WORKS

Apel, Willi, *Harvard Dictionary of Music*. Cambridge, Massachusetts: Harvard University Press, 1944. A very wide and detailed coverage of all aspects of music with only incidental biographical data.

Apel, Willi, and Ralph T. Daniel, *The Harvard Brief Dictionary of Music*. Cambridge, Massachusetts: Harvard University Press, 1960. An abridged and revised version of its parent volume.

*Baker's Biographical Dictionary of Musicians*, Fifth Edition, revised by Nicolas Slonimsky. New York: G. Schirmer, Inc., 1958. A standard reference book of biographical data. Includes lists of compositions and has some bibliographical material.

Scholes, Percy A., *The Concise Oxford Dictionary of Music*. London and New York: Oxford University Press, 1952. A handy volume, comprehensively covering music.

Scholes, Percy A., *The Oxford Companion to Music*, Ninth Edition. New York and London: Oxford University Press, 1955. The latest edition of a valuable reference work. Includes numerous illustrations, tables, and charts.

Thompson, Oscar, *The International Cyclopedia of Music and Musicians*, Seventh Edition, revised by Nicolas Slonimsky. New York: Dodd, Mead, and Company, 1949. An excellent one-volume encyclopedia which includes opera plots, pronunciations of names and titles, and a 282-page bibliography.

Westrup, J. A. and F. L. Harrison, *The New College Encyclopedia of Music*. New York: W. W. Norton & Company, Inc., 1960. A brief, yet comprehensive, small reference work which includes biographical data, terms, and commentaries on musical works.

## BOOKS ON MUSIC LITERATURE AND APPRECIATION

Bernstein, Martin, *An Introduction to Music*, Second Edition. New York: Prentice-Hall, Inc., 1951. An historical approach to the study of musical literature with biographical data and analyses of representative works.

Darrell, R. D., *Good Listening*. New York: New American Library, 1955, or Mentor. A convenient, inexpensive paper-back guide to music appreciation, literature, and history, originally published in a hardback edition by Alfred A. Knopf, Inc. Designed for the novice.

Erickson, Robert, *The Structure of Music: A Listener's Guide*. New York: The Noonday Press, 1959. An uncommonly enlightened and penetrating guide to listening through a study of musical texture.

Fleming, William, and Abraham Veinus, *Understanding Music*. New York: Henry Holt and Company, 1958. A well-written introduction to music for the inquiring adult. Approaches music through structure, style, and history. Excellent treatment of the composer and his relation to his materials, his product, the allied arts, and the world.

Machlis, Joseph, *The Enjoyment of Music*. New York: W. W. Norton & Company, Inc., 1955. A popular textbook on music appreciation which starts with the familiar and proceeds to the unfamiliar. Some biographical treatment of composers.

Newman, William S., *Understanding Music*, Second Edition. New York: Harper & Brothers, 1961. A mature and engaging introduction to music's elements, styles, and forms for both the layman and practitioner. Does not "talk down" to the reader. Takes its point of departure from the actual musical example. Excellent diagrams, charts, and appendices.

Siegmeister, Elie, *Invitation to Music*. Irvington-on-Hudson, N.Y.: Harvey House, 1961. A delightful and authoritative account of the development of music from antiquity to the present, supplemented by the author's own explanations on a record of the same name: Folkways FT 3603.

## HISTORIES OF MUSIC

Beekman, C. Cannon, Alvin H. Johnson, and William G. Waite, *The Art of Music*. New York: Thomas Y. Crowell Co., 1960. A scholarly short history of musical styles and ideas.

Einstein, Alfred, *A Short History of Music*, Fourth American Edition, revised. New York: Vintage Books, 1954. An inexpensive paper-back edition of the original hard-cover book published by Alfred A. Knopf, Inc. A remarkable condensation of the subject by an outstanding authority.

Ferguson, Donald N., *A History of Musical Thought*, Revised Edition. New York: Appleton-Century-Crofts, Inc., 1948. A standard history of music in Western culture.

Grout, Donald J., *A History of Western Music*. New York: W. W. Norton & Company, Inc., 1960. A distinguished and complete survey of Western art music. The history of musical style presented through music itself. Includes numerous examples, illustrations, and correlated lists for further reading and listening.

Lang, Paul Henry, *Music in Western Civilization*. New York: W. W. Norton & Company, Inc., 1941. An exhaustive and scholarly treatment of music history, correlating music with cultural and general history by an outstanding musicologist.

Leichtentritt, Hugo, *Everybody's Little History of Music*. New York: Associated Music Publishers, Inc., 1938. A popular paper-bound history of music by an eminent authority.

McKinney, Howard D., and W. R. Anderson, *Music in History: The Evolution of an Art*. New York: American Book Co., Inc., 1949. A survey emphasizing the correlation of music with cultural history and the history of the other arts.

Miller, Hugh M., *History of Music: A Survey from Ancient Times to the Present*, Third Edition. New York: Barnes & Noble, Inc., 1960. A concise paper-bound volume in the College Outline Series.

Sachs, Curt, *Our Musical Heritage*. New York: Prentice-Hall, Inc., 1955. A survey, particularly valuable for its treatment of primitive music.

## HARMONY AND MUSICIANSHIP TEXTS

Bauman, Alvin, and Charles W. Walton, *Elementary Musicianship*, Revised Edition. Englewood Cliffs, N. J.: Prentice-Hall, Inc., 1959. An excellent study of music structure using music as its point of departure. Designed for the beginner.

Dallin, Leon, *Foundations in Music Theory*. Belmont, Calif.: Wadsworth Publishing Company, Inc., 1962.

Elliot, Raymond, *Fundamentals of Music*. New York: Prentice-Hall, Inc., 1955. A vocal approach to rudiments, music reading, and melodic ear-training.

McHose, Allen I., *Basic Principles of the Technique of 18th and 19th Century Composition*. New York: Appleton-Century-Crofts, Inc., 1951. A thorough and systematic treatment of traditional harmonic practice.

Murphy, Howard A., and Edwin J. Stringham, *Creative Harmony and Musicianship*. Englewood Cliffs, N.J.: Prentice-Hall, Inc., 1951. A musical approach to the study of structure through writing, playing, listening, analysis, reading, and creative work.

Piston, Walter, *Harmony*, Revised Edition. New York: W. W. Norton & Co., Inc., 1948. A logical and systematic standard text for the study of traditional harmony.

## BOOKS ON RECORDED MUSIC

Cohn, Arthur, *The Collector's Twentieth Century Music in the Western Hemisphere*. Philadelphia and New York: J. B. Lippincott Company, 1961.

Grunfeld, Frederic V., editor, *Music and Recordings*. New York: Oxford University Press, 1955.

*The Guide to Long Playing Records*. Three volumes. New York: Alfred A. Knopf, Inc., 1955. See below at Kolodin, Miller, Schoenberg.

Hall, David and Abner Levin, *The Disc Book*. New York: Long Player Publications, Inc., 1955.

Hoops, Roy H., Jr. and Ray Lindstrom, editors, *Building Your Record Library*. New York: McGraw-Hill Book Co., 1956.

Kolodin, Irving, *Orchestral Music*. One of three volumes of *The Guide to Long Playing Records*. New York: Alfred A. Knopf, Inc., 1955.

Miller, Philip L., *Vocal Music*. One of three volumes of *The Guide to Long Playing Records*. New York: Alfred A. Knopf, Inc., 1955.

Schoenberg, H. C., *Chamber and Solo Instrumental Music*. One of three volumes of *The Guide to Long Playing Records*. New York: Alfred A. Knopf, Inc., 1955.

Taubman, Howard, *How to Build a Record Library*. Garden City, N.Y.: Hanover House, 1956.

# Index